TAKING CARE
of YOUR OWN

THE GRAND ROUNDS PRESS

TAKING CARE
of YOUR OWN

PERRI KLASS, M.D.

WHITTLE DIRECT BOOKS

THE GRAND ROUNDS PRESS

The Grand Rounds Press presents original short books by distinguished authors on subjects of importance to the medical profession.

The series is edited and published by Whittle Books, a business unit of Whittle Communications L.P. A new book is published approximately every three months. The series reflects a broad spectrum of responsible opinions. In each book the opinions expressed are those of the author, not the publisher or advertiser.

I welcome your comments on this unique endeavor.

William S. Rukeyser
Editor in Chief

Library of Congress Catalog Card Number: 92-81406
Klass, Perri, M.D.
Taking Care of Your Own
ISBN: 1-879736-08-X
ISSN: 1053-6620

I would like to thank all the people
who spoke to me about their experiences as the children
of doctors, as doctors themselves, and as parents.
I am grateful to Elizabeth Barnett,
Anne Breña, Eileen Costello, Sarah Feldman, Steve Goldstein,
Daniel Wayne Harris and Jo-Ann S. Harris, Daniel McQuillen,
Robert Needlman, and Pam Wendell,
as well as to numerous people who
contributed anonymously.

I N T R O D U C T I O N 11

C H A P T E R   O N E
Pregnancy 14

C H A P T E R   T W O
Labor and Delivery 24

C H A P T E R   T H R E E
Your Patients, Your Children 34

C H A P T E R   F O U R
When They Get Sick 46

C H A P T E R   F I V E
Your Parents, Your Doctors 56

C H A P T E R   S I X
Time and Timing 65

C O N C L U S I O N 74

INTRODUCTION

person becomes a parent simply by having a child. No training is required, no degree or certification is given. There is, of course, on-the-job training that continues for a lifetime.

In learning how to raise children, parents depend on many sources of information and advice, ranging from their own parents and friends to books (and nowadays, videotapes) put out by experts on child-rearing. This information is filtered through the specifics of your own background, socioeconomic class, religious beliefs, and cultural context. All will shape how you raise a child, the goals you set for yourself, and the day-to-day results you achieve. There is no one rule book to master, no test you must pass.

In contrast, to become a doctor, you have to pass test after test just to earn the right to enter training. During that training, you are constantly judged and tested and graded. New skills are forced upon you. Your qualification is finally marked with a ceremony, a degree—and the necessity for further training.

And yet the two processes overlap in various ways, some metaphorical and others eminently concrete. Both are transformations, and both roles are identities rather than occupations. You don't work as a doctor, you *are* a doctor; the profession is generally perceived (by doctors and by others) as a lifelong commitment. You are seen as a doctor 24 hours a day, whether or not you are actually working. Every doctor who has ever been asked for advice at a party or spent a family wedding listening to a relative's long account of his symptoms knows this.

Similarly, once a parent, always a parent. Becoming a parent entails another fundamental change in how you identify yourself and how the world identifies you.

Either identity, doctor or parent, can be a complete, full-time, all-absorbing job. There are people for whom being a doctor is all-consuming; life has no room for anything else. And there are people who approach parenthood in the same way. Those of us who struggle with the interesting project of stretching our lives to include some satisfactory version of both roles (as well as perhaps another ingredient or two) often find ourselves measuring each separate identity against an ideal built on the assumption that the job can be done right only by a truly devoted full-timer.

Both roles involve caretaking and the weight of heavy responsibility—literal life-and-death responsibility. There is terrible anxiety about making a mistake when you have been entrusted with someone's well-being, and the difficult lesson to be learned that uncertainty is unavoidable and ambiguity can never be eliminated, however good your intentions, however rigorous your preparation, however intense your dedication.

Doctor and parent are both authority figures, set somewhere on a spectrum that ranges from traditional to less traditional. Both must contend with the wish to appear omniscient and omnipotent—and with the reality that their knowledge and powers are limited, and that those limitations will inevitably be discovered.

In writing and thinking about the connections between medicine and parenthood (the two most important experiences of my own adult life), I looked for the ways in which parenthood affects doctors, and the ways in which the practice of medicine affects parental behavior. In the words and writings of other physicians, in the images of physicians in fiction from our own time and 100 years ago, in the sociologic, psychiatric, and medical literature, I looked for descriptions of parents as doctors, doctors as parents.

This book begins with pregnancy and traces the experience of the physician who is also a parent through labor and delivery and into the children's infancy and childhood. I chose to spend a fair amount of time on the issues that kept coming up when I spoke to doctors and to their children. The first of these was, What happens when a doctor's child gets sick? How do parents handle it when their professional expertise becomes involved in questions relating to their own offspring? What happens to the emotional safeguards that protect doctors from some of the pain experienced by their patients?

Second was the question of time. How can there be time enough in one life for medicine and also for parenthood? And how is that time distributed, both within a day—as doctors struggle with the nitty-gritty of daily life—and throughout a lifetime in the medical profession? When do you have your children, and how do you set up your professional life so that you have room to maneuver?

I am deeply grateful to all the physicians and children of physicians (sometimes one and the same person) who took the time to speak to me and who allowed me to quote family memories and personal emotions. Almost all of them, once they got going, were eager to put into words, sometimes for the first time, their feelings about some of the basic issues that have shaped their lives.

There is not a large literature on the experience of being a doctor's child, or of being a doctor with children. Certain aspects have been comparatively well studied—the experience of pregnancy during residency, for example. But Dr. David Maddison, writing in *The Medical Journal of Australia* in 1974, commented that the experience of being part of a doctor's family is "an area in which we have to rely almost entirely on impressionistic evidence" because there have been so few studies done. That is still largely true today. Perhaps it is time for us as a profession to look more closely at our family lives, to look for what they can tell us about the consequences of our professional training, the personal ramifications of the jobs we do, and what they say about who we are.

CHAPTER ONE

PREGNANCY

I had no clue what it was like to be pregnant—as a resident I was very blinded. Patients often complained to nurses about pelvic pain, nosebleeds, gum bleeds, but not to the doctor. I had never heard anyone complain that breastfeeding hurts. As obstetricians, we see patients six weeks postpartum, and it doesn't hurt by then. When I started nursing, I called everyone I know. I called the La Leche League. I was really shocked, but I discovered this pain was fairly standard.

The pure joy I get as an obstetrician delivering someone else's baby has increased tremendously—it's like my own daughter is born again. Tears come to my eyes every time.

—Obstetrician, age 31

t is not easy to be pregnant during residency. It is, quite frankly, not even easy to *get* pregnant during residency. Right before my internship began in 1986, the hospital held a picnic to welcome all the new interns, complete with a hot dog roast and an ostentatiously convivial softball game between residents and attendings. Soon after I arrived with Larry and our son, Benjamin, Larry was approached by the husband of one of the interns who was just completing her year. The husband's self-appointed mission was to tell each incoming nonphysician husband or boyfriend, "Say goodbye to your sex life, here and now."

When you plan a pregnancy during residency, you cross-reference your call schedule with your menstrual cycle, and cross-reference both with your wheel of fortune, that little plastic disc that lets you calculate EDC for any given date of conception. *Let's see now,* you say to yourself, *if we want to try for a baby in January, when I'll be doing my elective time, I need to conceive in April. But I'm in the*

NICU in April, and that's every third night on call in the hospital. So let's see then, I ought to be ovulating on the fifth, you mutter, *but I'm on call that night. So there's the sixth, when I'm post-call and I'll probably be comatose, and our best bet might be the fourth, when I'm out of the hospital on swing . . .*

Conceiving during residency can seem like a victory for the forces of life and libido over the tyranny of call schedules and ridiculous working hours. It can also seem like a victory of the biological imperative over common sense; why would anyone in her right mind choose these particular years to have a baby? We all know some of the answers, of course. The middle twenties to early thirties are prime childbearing years for women, many of whom have already deferred having children while preparing for medical school, getting through medical school. As residents, they are finally earning salaries, however small, rather than paying heavy tuition. Their partners may also be reaching new levels of professional security.

But more important than any arguments about financial status or marital stages, I suspect, is the fact that medical training is long, arduous, and replete with delayed gratification. Having a baby can come to seem like one joy you are not going to let them deny you, one important decision you are going to make for yourself during these years when so many are made for you, one gratification too essential to delay any further.

My first child was conceived at the end of my first year in medical school and born in the middle of my second. I went into labor while studying for my endocrinology exam, which was scheduled for the day after my due date. I knew I could not afford to take the risk of not preparing for the exam; if I didn't study, counting on the baby as my *deus ex machina*, I would certainly not go into labor until the exam was over. On the other hand, I thought with some irritation, if I put time and effort into learning the disorders of the thyroid and the parathyroid, I would undoubtedly go into labor, miss the exam, forget everything I had learned, and have to start again from scratch to take the makeup. So I started studying, and I went into labor and gave birth on my due date, the day before the exam.

Being pregnant in medical school turned out to be something of a seminal (no pun intended) experience for me. It was the first time in a long time that I had been under any kind of medical care, and that led to a sudden confusion of roles. I became a patient while struggling to see myself as a doctor, and I found myself feeling angry about the way reproductive medicine was being taught in medical school. The course seemed to stress only the million and one terrible things that could go wrong and treated pregnancy as dangerous and often pathological. It made me angry to hear obstetricians talking as if they controlled labor and delivery when I was so determined as a patient (a privileged, entitled, educated, demanding patient, of course) to make as many of my own decisions as possible.

I seriously considered a home delivery. I went out of my way to seek out the doctor most committed to forgoing unnecessary interventions. He didn't use ultrasound to check the fetal heart rate; he used a fetoscope. I was 24, so I didn't need amniocentesis. The delivery would be in a community hospital with no residents on the premises. No interventions, no ultrasound, no genetic screening, no residents. I saw these refusals, I suppose, as defiances, as rejections I would hurl into the face of the medical establishment, perhaps as a way to hold on to my identity as my training proceeded.

In my confusion and arrogance, I wrote and published an article about having a baby while in medical school; I complained that I had learned nothing about healthy pregnancy and natural childbirth. Lots of doctors got angry. I got letters telling me I would be glad enough of medical interventions when my baby got into trouble. Some of my classmates were angry too, feeling that their training was being criticized.

I had my second child five years later, right at the end of my residency. I knew a lot more by then: I had been to lots of deliveries, had resuscitated babies, and had waited for babies known to have congenital anomalies to be born. I had cared for my share of 28-week preemies, and 26-weekers, and by the end of my residency, 24-weekers. These were years during which the medical profession was moving back the frontier of survival so that younger and younger premature babies had a better and better chance of surviving, a consequence of spectacularly dramatic medical intervention. I knew what to do in the delivery room for gastroschisis (wrap the exposed intestines gently in gauze soaked in sterile saline, cover with plastic wrap to prevent heat and water loss, then call the surgeons). I knew what choanal atresia looked like (can't pass the DeLee tube down through the nose to the stomach) and what associated anomalies to look for (the CHARGE association: *C* is for coloboma, *H* is for heart . . .). I had become, unquestionably, a foot soldier in the great march of medical interventions. I was in favor of early Cesarean sections so I wouldn't have to hang around the DR watching the monitor and worrying. I was in favor of scalp

"Come here! Hurry! There are little animals in this rain water... They swim! They play around! They are a thousand times smaller than any creatures we can see with our eyes alone...Look! See what I have discovered."

Miles is proud to present this series on...

Powerful Innovators

Powerful Innovator

Anton van Leeuwenhoek (1632-1723)

Although others had already created microscopes, Leeuwenhoek's lenses possessed such clarity and magnification power that he helped the world see those "little animals."

Leeuwenhoek's achievements are particularly impressive since he had little education and certainly no scientific training. His life's passion: creating the most powerful magnification possible.

Leeuwenhoek was the first person to see protozoa and bacteria, and he gave the first clear description of capillary circulation. He enthusiastically reported his findings on muscle, teeth scrapings, hair, skin, and fleas, much to the amazement of the British Royal Society, whose skepticism turned into respect after Leeuwenhoek sent each member a lens.

Powerful Antimicrobial

Is it speed...or power...or both that are important in the hospital? If it's speed, then there is no antimicrobial faster than Cipro® in killing in vitro.* And if it's power, none of the major intravenous antimicrobials compares with Cipro® in its broad coverage of gram-negative and gram-positive pathogens...in its in vitro potency...in its postantibiotic effect. So when you want something fast and powerful...Cipro® I.V.

Cipro® I.V. is indicated for mild to moderate lower respiratory, skin and skin structure, and bone and joint infections, and mild, moderate, severe, and complicated urinary tract infections.†

The most potent fluoroquinolone.[1-3]*

See complete prescribing information at the end of this book.

Powerful Numbers

speak for themselves:

2... *The number of hours ciprofloxacin needed for complete killing* in vitro *of a representative isolate of* Pseudomonas aeruginosa, *a rate that was more than two times faster than that of ceftazidime, piperacillin, imipenem, or tobramycin.**

4... *The number of stages of cell growth during which ciprofloxacin actively kills— the lag, exponential growth, stationary, and dying-off phases.**

96... *The percent susceptibility of 71,389 clinical isolates of* Enterobacteriaceae *to ciprofloxacin.**

Cipro® I.V.
(ciprofloxacin)

The most potent fluoroquinolone. [1-3]*

*In vitro activity does not necessarily imply a correlation with *in vivo* results.
†Due to susceptible strains of indicated pathogens. See indicated organisms in prescribing information.

See complete prescribing information at the end of this book.

MILES
Pharmaceutical Division

Miles Inc.
Pharmaceutical Division
400 Morgan Lane
West Haven, CT 06516

pH's and episiotomies—anything to reassure me, anything to get the baby out.

No delivery that I attended as a pediatrician was anything like my own son's birth had been. Even when the baby happened to pop out healthy and vigorous (common enough when you're called to the delivery room for occasional decels), I never did for those babies what the doctor had done for my own son: wrap him in a blanket and hand him to his mother. No, I was the pediatrician; I had a job to do. The baby went on the warming table and I suctioned and examined and assigned Apgars, usually remembering to call over to the parents some reassuring comment about how well their baby was doing. This, I thought, marked me as one of the sensitive ones.

To my surprise, when I contemplated my second pregnancy I found I had developed a new medical paranoia. I was still afraid of medical interventions, but it was no longer a fear centered on my wish for a natural, beautiful birth experience and for a successful mother-baby bonding. Along with all the other pediatric residents, I had become very impatient with people who worried about bonding while I was worrying about oxygenation. Instead, I worried that I would have a baby born too early, or a baby born asphyxiated, and the pediatricians would rush in and resuscitate. I knew too much about those interventions by then, and I was afraid of having a baby whose whole survival would be a continuing medical drama, whose future would be a medical question mark.

In the teaching hospital where I trained, there was essentially no such thing as a stillbirth. Except in the case of a well-documented intrauterine fetal demise, the obstetricians' reaction to a baby born without a heart rate was to call the pediatricians. We muttered about how the whole point was to make an obstetrical loss into a pediatric problem, but we went; we intubated and resuscitated all those babies. In residency, we all learned over and over the story of the child with Apgars of zero, zero, one, and two: Zero at one minute because born limp and blue and without a heart rate. Zero at five minutes—resuscitation under way, but not yet successful. One at 10 minutes—the baby has a heart rate, but it's less than 100. And so on.

That was my nightmare. I figured it would be less likely to happen at a community hospital than at a teaching center. I was avoiding my colleagues, and especially avoiding the neonatologists. At my first appointment with the obstetrician, a woman I chose because I had worked with her as a medical student and liked her style, I marched into the office and informed her that I wanted her to promise me that if I had a stillborn baby, there would be no resuscitation. When I later mentioned this conversation to one of the emergency room attendings at the hospital where I was a resident, he told me matter-of-factly that the real reason he had wanted to be in the delivery room when his children were born was so he could throw himself in front of the neonatologist if it looked like there was going to be a code.

So that was what three years of pediatric residency did to me. I had a much more medicalized pregnancy the second time around, partly because I was older and therefore more legitimately at risk, and partly because I was paranoid about so many things. When I had my amniocentesis, I asked to be tested for cystic fibrosis and muscular dystrophy. Neither is in my family or in Larry's, but I had seen so many kids with both diseases that I thought of them as common, as likely to occur—even as more probable than a truly healthy baby.

> *When I was pregnant with my first child, during my fellowship, I didn't worry. I would go in and examine kids with congenital CMV. I didn't allow anything to cross my mind other than a normal pregnancy, a normal baby. With my second child it was different. I had lost two babies in between—miscarriages—and I knew things could go wrong.*
>
> —Pediatrician, age 42

For many doctors and residents, pregnancy brings added concerns about teratogenic exposures and dangerous infections. You want to stay away from the radiology suite. You don't want to be in the ribavirin room. You worry about being exposed to CMV or HIV. Most pregnant doctors try to avoid radiation and potentially teratogenic substances and take extra precautions with regard to infections. But you don't refuse to examine babies just because some of them may have congenital CMV. You gown and glove and wash your hands, that's all. Then you wake up in the middle of the night and wash them again.

I drew blood and started IVs right through my second pregnancy, and many of the patients were HIV-positive. I'm not sure I would do that again; I think I'd rather pass my pregnancy without that particular anxiety. However, I was a resident then, and I didn't think I had the choice.

One night, I was the senior in the ICU and had to send someone for a stat CT scan. I was three or four months pregnant and hadn't yet told anyone at the hospital. Normal etiquette called for me to leave the junior in charge of the ICU and take the guy over to CT myself. Instead I told the junior resident that he would have to go, and I told him why. He was nice about it. I remember one other time I was going up from the ER with a kid who turned out to need another holder for the neck films, and I recruited a passing resident. Now, I could have worn the lead apron, but the fact is, I had no idea what was safe and what wasn't, and I had no desire to run even the ghost of a risk.

Hospitals are full of risks, and there are precautions observed with more or less care. But there is always the X-ray tech who comes to the NICU in the middle of the night to take a portable chest film and calls out "X-ray!" as the film is taken instead of a minute before, so no one has a chance to step out of range. And there is the senior resident, called to start an IV on a seriously ill child who has already suffered through four attempts by two interns, who finds herself tearing off the index finger of her left glove to feel for the tiny, elusive vein, or maybe even strips off both gloves, muttering something apologetic about how she's better without them.

There are dirty needles around and infectious exposures, not just HIV and hepatitis B, but also meningococcus, say, or RSV. I think the thing I worried about most was not that I would stick myself with a needle and actually contract HIV (which is, after all, a fairly low risk); I was concerned that I would stick myself and then have to *worry* about HIV, that it would cast a shadow over my pregnancy, a shadow of blame and anxiety at having already failed in my most basic maternal responsibility to protect my passenger. A hospital can be a scary place to work (as can many kinds of medical practices) if seen through the cautious eyes of a pregnant woman.

So you worry about keeping your baby safe while you're pregnant and, in pediatrics at least, you think about your delivery room experience. You think about premature births, and as you move through the pregnancy, you imagine the result of going into labor at each point. Ask a pediatrician when his baby is due, and you get an answer like, "My wife's 28 weeks now, so I'm starting to relax— 28-weekers do okay. Not like a 26-weeker."

If you work in NICUs, you often come to have very strong feelings about the borderline babies, the ones almost too small to live. Like many people who have had a lot of exposure to NICUs, I came to believe that I would not want a very tiny preemie kept alive, just as I would not want a stillborn baby resuscitated. I don't believe that every wanted pregnancy has to end in a live birth. I believe there is such a thing as a baby born too small to live, or a baby born dead. This is just another way of saying that I don't think I would want a baby of mine put through extremely aggressive medical manipulations if there was a chance the baby would be left with severe sequelae. It is my mandate as a pediatrician to take care of handicapped children, but I am troubled by the consequences of our determination to prevent miscarriage and stillbirth at any cost.

With the influx of more and more women into medicine, pregnancy among residents has become a relatively common event. For pregnant residents, there is first and foremost the problem of scheduling: factoring maternity leave into a schedule already too tight and too demanding, figuring out who will do the extra call nights, deciding how long the new mother will get to spend with her baby before she returns to working a resident's schedule.

In 1988, obstetrician Sharon T. Phelan surveyed 2,000 American women who had recently completed residencies in ob-gyn, surgery, and psychiatry and found that among the married women, pregnancy was quite common during residency: the rates were 49 percent for ob-gyns, 44 percent for psychiatrists, and 38 percent for surgeons. Phelan's study (as well as several others) found that the pregnancies tended to be planned.

A study published by Dr. Mark Klebanoff and others in 1990 (to be discussed in detail in a later chapter) found that pregnancy rates among female residents were only slightly lower than pregnancy rates among the wives of their male colleagues. And in fact, whether they have their children during residency or later (or earlier), most physicians, male and female, will have children. For all the upheavals that children bring into life, male physicians can approach fatherhood with relatively little obvious drama. But at some point, a woman's medical career (like her elastic-waisted skirts) has to stretch to accommodate pregnancy, childbirth, and everything that comes after.

For the female physician, pregnancy can also cause work-related stress. In many studies, women reported lack of support—if not outright hostility—from co-workers and supervisors. This may be especially true during residency, when a pregnant colleague may be seen as a walking, breathing harbinger of extra nights on call for others. Hospital residency programs may reluctantly permit a mandated maternity leave but require the other residents to work extra nights on call instead of hiring more help. Those residents are given to understand that their colleague, at home postpartum with her newborn, is the one to blame; naturally they won't be sending flowers or knitting booties.

Dr. Kathleen Franco and her colleagues studied clinical faculty members and residents at the Medical College of Ohio in Toledo in 1982. Of those who responded to the questionnaire, 80 percent felt that "a pregnant colleague caused them personal inconvenience." A similarly large number reported inconvenience to their department. However, 68 percent believed that "the presence of a pregnant colleague would have a positive or humanizing effect on the work environment." The majority of those who answered the survey agreed with the idea that special arrangements should be made for a pregnant colleague (but this received less support among residents than among faculty members). And a study by Dr. Maureen Sayres found that although resident pregnancy was not at all rare, only one-fifth of the residency programs surveyed had a maternity-leave policy.

One reason for the problems of pregnant residents may be that many in the medical profession are still in a state of profound denial. Yes, residency slots are filled with young women of childbearing age. And yes, year after year these young women decide to take on the additional responsibilities of having and raising children. But somehow, the maternity-leave policies still are not in place, and those who administer residency programs resolutely refuse to build in the kind of flexibility that would allow the programs to absorb a pregnancy or two along the way.

Dr. M. Andrew Greganti and Dr. Suzanne W. Fletcher, writing in the editorial section of the *Annals of Internal Medicine* in 1985, dissected the reasons for this apparent reluctance to deal with reality. First of all, they said, it would be troublesome to adapt residency programs to accommodate pregnancy. It is easier to view the pregnancy and its attendant reschedulings as the woman's own responsibility, to punish her, in a certain sense, for allowing anything else to compete with what should be an all-consuming task—her residency. The authors summed up: "As the percentage of women in internal-medicine residency programs continues to increase, this approach will become progressively less tenable. . . . Many women residents are having families, thus forcing attention, willingly or not, from those responsible for residency training programs. Finally, maintaining the current state of affairs is inconsistent with recent attempts to make residency training more congruous with personal and 'human' needs."

In 1981, Johanna Shapiro of the University of California Irvine Medical Center published a study of residents' attitudes toward having children during residency. Both male and female residents felt that it was harder for female than for male residents to balance their careers with parenthood. However, more of the female residents felt that male residents should postpone having children until after residency than felt that female residents should do so, while the male residents tended to feel that the female residents should be the ones to wait. Both male and female residents agreed that their departments had a more favorable attitude toward the man with a pregnant wife than toward the pregnant female resident. Although they identified these biases, the doctors surveyed were not eager to legislate corrections. "In general," the authors concluded, "suggested policies for the pregnant resident were only slightly more generous than toward the resident with a pregnant spouse."

Residency can serve here as a microcosm of medical existence: the best of times, and the worst of times. The problems that reach an almost insane pitch in residency are present in one form or another throughout most medical careers. Can you work long hours when you're pregnant? Are you willing to take certain risks, or can you change your behavior enough to reduce them by taking precautions? Will having a baby mean someone has to cover for you, and who, and for how long, and how will you pay it back? Will you be letting down your colleagues, letting down your patients? And will you ever again offer medicine the same clear, unadulterated attention and loyalty, the same devotion, the same dedication?

Dr. Elizabeth L. Auchincloss, writing in a 1982 issue of the *American Journal of Psychiatry*, offered a description of a conflict that arose in a psychiatric residency program when three of 12 second-year residents became pregnant. Although the first woman's pregnancy and maternity leave seemed to go smoothly, hostility erupted when she found she could not return to work full time, leaving eight additional nights on call to be divided among her colleagues. The male residents decided those call nights would be the responsibility of the other two pregnant women. The author reported: "Both sides entered the meeting with tempers flaring. The men and the pregnant women (who had the support of the other women) expressed much hostility toward each other. Not until these hostile feelings were expressed and explored could the remaining on-call nights be divided and peace be established. All of the residents were shaken by the amount of anger generated by the events and expressed at the meeting."

That the expression and exploration of those feelings was seen as desirable probably had much to do with the discipline: psychiatry residents might be expected to see the value of such discussion. Similarly, the author's analysis might seem arcane to those in other branches of medicine. She suggested, among other things, that the reactions of the men to the pregnant women included expressions of anger, envy, and competition, all of which are defined in the psychoanalytic literature as part of woman-envy and pregnancy-envy. "These feelings are based on either the little boy's notion that his pregnant mother possesses an enviable, large penis or on his more primitive envy of the omnipotent, controlling pre-oedipal mother, the possessor of powerful secrets. Some authors have suggested that these feelings are more intense among physicians and others in nurturing or creative professions."

It would be fascinating, not to say delightful, to see a pregnant resident in a surgical program, or even in internal medicine, with the self-confidence (one could not say the balls, however appropriate) to offer this explanation to her program director.

Auchincloss summed up the pregnant resident's dilemma well, and not just for psychiatry: "A normal, expectable life event creates for her a situation of deviance in which she must either ask for special help or, resenting this, make angry demands."

CHAPTER TWO

LABOR AND DELIVERY

I had decided I would ask for an epidural. Basically, I had never had a patient who had one say she didn't like it. So when I was three centimeters dilated, I thought, I'll just be smarter than the average patient, I'll ask early. Of course I got special treatment. They wanted me to feel good quickly, maybe gave me a heavy dose—and I hated it. I couldn't move, felt like I couldn't breathe and was lying there cemented down. I wanted to be in control so much that I demanded the epidural—and then I couldn't stand being out of control. I am the only person I know who had an epidural who wouldn't have one again. Everyone always says, Oh, it was so great, it was God's gift. But I waited till it wore off to push, and I felt much better. After the delivery I was able to get up and walk to the bathroom, and I left the next day.

—Obstetrician, age 31

f pregnancy teaches doctors about being patients, labor and delivery teach them about being hospitalized, about the remarkable loss of power that comes with the johnny and the ID bracelet. They also teach what a multitude of medical procedures feel like from the other side. On the most trivial level, I was shocked by the size of the IV catheters used in adults: in pediatrics, we are used to tiny 22- and 24-gauge catheters; a 20-gauge looks like a big pipe. When I was hospitalized for the birth of my daughter, Josephine, I was shocked to have a nurse matter-of-factly start a 16-gauge IV in my hand. I just couldn't imagine why she needed anything so enormous.

On a deeper level, the issue of who is in control takes on special complexity when a doctor is a patient. In obstetrics, there is a trade-off between pain control and power; if you have anesthesia, you give up control of your body. For some of us, that turns out to be more terrifying than pain. When I was pregnant with my first child, I thought the reason I was so determined to have a completely natural birth had to do with wanting what was best for my baby (no drugs, no unproven interventions) and perhaps with my natural-is-better value system. I now suspect that it had more to do with one of the personality traits that sent me into the medical profession: I like to be in charge. While I don't mind doing medical things to others, I hate having them done to me.

I had learned the first time around that I hate being a patient in a hospital, even a nice hospital with nice, kind, sympathetic nurses and cheerful paintings on the walls of the birthing room. I hate it, I hate it, I hate it. I was ready to go home four hours after the birth, the hospital's minimum for "early discharge." As it happened, it had been a long and hard first labor (more than 24 hours), with a prolonged pushing phase. I had lost a fair amount of blood and was exhausted. The doctor suggested that I consider staying overnight, and though I have no clear recollection of it, Larry tells me I began arguing—sounding remarkably cogent and pulled together—from the birthing-room bed. What were they going to do for me in the hospital that couldn't be done at home? Did they really think I had lost so much blood that I was going to need a transfusion? How was my blood pressure? If I took it easy and drank plenty of liquids, couldn't I be on my way?

And so we got out of there. I can still remember the relief, the joy of being helped up my own icy steps and collapsing with my baby in my own bedroom. Everyone in the hospital was nice, and everyone meant well, and they had taken good care of me. But I felt as though I had just successfully tunneled out of Sing Sing.

By the time the second baby came around, hospitals had become my native ground, places that felt reassuring and safe. Yes, things can go wrong, but if they do, then something can be done. In a hospital, there's wall oxygen, a crash cart right outside the door, and lots of people who know what they're doing. Residency teaches you as graphically as possible the benefits of having the equipment you need and the people who know how to use it.

Interestingly, I did not find that this knowledge translated over when I once again found myself a patient, nine months pregnant. True, I was no longer absolutely determined to resist any and all interventions for the sake of staying natural. For one thing, I had absorbed some of the prevailing attitude that people who were extremely "natural" were a little bit nuts, like the woman whose baby had dangerously high hyperbilirubinemia. The baby was under double bili lights in the newborn intensive care unit, with every possible inch of his skin exposed to the ultraviolet lights in hopes of breaking down the bilirubin and sparing him the dangers of an exchange transfusion. All this had been explained to his mother, who was an educated and cooperative woman. But when the NICU nurse went to the child's bedside, the mother was found with her great big adult-sized hands interposed between his skin and the bili lights, massaging her baby. She was not just holding his hand or touching him, but kneading his back and shoulders, covering his bottom. When she was reminded that he really needed to be exposed to the lights, she explained that by massaging him and reciting his mantra, she was actually doing much more for him than the bili lights could.

So by the time my second baby was due, I was a lot more self-conscious about the ideology and vocabulary of totally natural birth. But I was still bound and determined to get out of that hospital after four hours. As it happened, I ended up requesting a particular intervention because my pregnancy went past my due date. This happens not infrequently, and it can simply mean that the due date was wrong. But not if you're a resident. I had no doubts about my due date, and I did not want a post-dates baby.

Once again, delivery room war stories were informing my thinking. Hanging around the NICU, waiting for the delivery room beeper to go off, we used to trade our theories, our fears, our own disasters, and the semiapocryphal, worst-case hospital legends. One of the things people used to say was, "I'd rather get a premature baby than a post-dates baby." Post-dates babies are scary; they're big, and they can come out looking awful if the placenta has deteriorated. And there's that awful sense that they were okay a couple of weeks ago and have withered on the vine. There was no way I was going to have a 43-weeker. I started to nag my obstetrician as soon as my due date had passed. To hell with natural; I wanted to be induced. And so, at a little more than a week past the due date, I was.

The first time around there had been no monitor, no IV, no drugs of any kind. Now, with a humongous adult-sized IV dripping Pitocin into my hand, there had to be a monitor. It was a very instructive experience, and it ended up reinforcing some of the dogma about natural childbirth I had more or less let slip. When I was in labor with no monitor, people paid attention to me, to how I was feeling and to what made the pain easier to handle. They intermittently listened to the fetal heart by fetoscope, and the rest of the time I walked around trying to divert myself.

Now, with Pitocin running in and a monitor around my belly, the monitor became the absolute and complete focus of the people taking care of me. The right position for me was the one that produced the clearest tracing. The nurse would come into the room and look not at me, but at the monitor.

I was finally allowed to get up and walk, but the portable monitor didn't transmit very well, which occasioned much concern. Finally, I lay down and watched an episode of *Divorce Court* that I suppose is now irreversibly printed on my consciousness. (It was about a husband who claimed he hadn't known before he married that his wife was a transsexual and who now wanted a divorce because she couldn't give him children. The wife claimed he had known all along about her sex-change operation and only wanted the divorce so that he could marry another woman, a sluttish, unprincipled little home-wrecker.)

The experience left me with a profound dislike of monitors, which, according to recent studies, have turned out to be very disappointing in terms of any clearly significant effect on the mortality and morbidity of newborns. Daytime television, however, may have significant potential as obstetrical anesthesia.

Anyway, I got out of the hospital once again at four hours with a healthy baby—and this time I had much more ammunition to use if anyone had a problem with my going home early. Wasn't I now a full-fledged pediatrician? Couldn't I be depended upon to watch my own baby for any problems that might arise? Gangway, I'm outta here.

My daughter was born when I was finishing the Ph.D. part of my M.D.-Ph.D. She was born after my wife was in labor on and off for four days. I couldn't remember any pediatrics, and I was absolutely terrified. The baby was fine, but she did need to be under bili lights, and I thought, I'll be starting residency in four months and if I am going to stay in the hospital all night with other people's children, then I am going to stay with my own. *So my first obsessive-compulsive physician behavior was to stay overnight with my child in the nursery with my hand in the warmer.*
—Pediatrician, age 35

It can be hard for doctors to give up control, hard to accept the million tiny indignities of hospitalization. You may find, looking at yourself in a johnny, that your reflection is a palimpsest of other patients, other people you have seen in that same garb in that same position. Those images are not necessarily comforting; they may remind you of illness, pain, suffering, and even death. Doctors are generally thought to make difficult patients: entitled, demanding, interfering, and unable to give up the one role and take on the other. But who *wouldn't* rather be the doctor than the patient?

It is also, to be honest, not all that easy to be the obstetrician or pediatrician who attends the labor and delivery of another doctor or a doctor's partner. I have a friend who was recently the chief resident of her pediatrics program and is married to another pediatrician. She had a baby not long ago, and the baby had some problems in the delivery room. "A resident came to the delivery, a senior from Hospital A," my friend reported. "I thought she did an excellent job with the resuscitation, but she probably should have been a little more organized. She did all the right things, but she just wasn't as smooth as she could have been." I suggested that maybe she had been flustered by the idea that she was doing this under the eyes of two colleagues. My friend's husband commented that he had actually been tempted to step in and take over at one point, but had restrained himself. It was obvious that he also felt he could have done it a little more smoothly.

When I was 26 weeks pregnant, I started having contractions. We ended up at the university hospital—I got transferred in under emergency conditions. There were two neonatology fellows there that night; one I had done my pediatrics residency with, and the other had been an intern with my husband. The one who knew my husband came in and tried telling him everything very intellectually— all about artificial surfactant, and how 26-weekers do better than they used to. And all the time her body language communicated that she thought we were up shit creek without a paddle if I went on to deliver.

Later, the guy I had trained with came in. I felt comfortable with the way he dealt with me, but I saw right through it. He was trying to reassure me, telling me 26-weekers do great, and I was thinking, I remember saying things like that to patients, and I wasn't reassured. And of course I was embarrassed, lying there half-naked with this guy I never really knew all that well. . . . Then, after

"I have worked as hard as I could... if my success has been greater than that of most...the reason is that I came in my wanderings through the medical field upon regions where the gold was still lying by the wayside...and that is of no great merit."

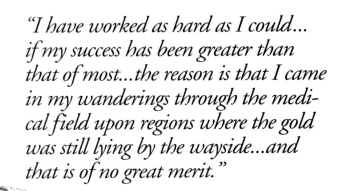

Miles is proud to present this series on...

Powerful Innovators

Powerful Physician

Robert Koch (1843-1910)

Even Koch himself would have been surprised to learn in 1866 that he would become one of the most important bacteriologists of all time. His dream of traveling to exotic ports took an ironic turn when his wife's gift of a microscope spurred his interest in the exotic world of microbes.

With a passionate interest in bacteriology generated by a crisis that struck in 1876 (an anthrax epidemic among local cattle), Koch studied the disease, cultured the organism on artificial media, analyzed its complete life cycle, and transferred the infection to mice.

Koch's research in bacteriology continued: He isolated and cultivated staphylococci from surgical infections, analyzed streptococci taken from wound exudate, and discovered the bacillus that causes conjunctivitis. Perhaps his most important contribution was the discovery of the bacillus responsible for tuberculosis, a devastating illness at that time.

Powerful Antimicrobial

Cipro® gives you the power you need to eradicate causative pathogens of skin infections.* With its excellent penetration of blister fluid,† Cipro® is <u>proven</u> effective monotherapy for many patients with skin/skin structure infections beyond the reach of traditional first-line antibiotics.‡

Cipro® TABLETS

(ciprofloxacin HCI)

The most potent fluoroquinolone.[1-3]§

* Due to susceptible strains of indicated pathogens. See indicated organisms in prescribing information.
† Tissue/fluid penetration is regarded as essential to therapeutic efficacy, but penetration levels have not been correlated with specific therapeutic results.
‡ *Physicians' Desk Reference®*. 46th ed. Oradell, NJ: Medical Economics Co Inc; 1992:575, 916, 1251, 1405, 2194, 2198.
§ *In vitro* activity does not necessarily imply a correlation with *in vivo* results.

See complete prescribing information at the end of this book.

Powerful Numbers

Speak for themselves

12 ...*Number of hours serum concentrations of Cipro® are maintained in excess of MIC$_{90s}$ of susceptible bacteria.*

40 ...*Cipro® peak skin blister fluid concentration is at least 40% higher than the MIC$_{90s}$ of most common bacteria.[†]*

96 ...*The percentage of favorable clinical response (resolution + improvement) with Cipro® reported in skin infections such as infected ulcer, postoperative wounds, cellulitis, infected burns, and abscesses.*

250/500/750 ...*Dosage strengths of Cipro® Tablets available.*

Cipro® TABLETS

(ciprofloxacin HCl)

The most potent fluoroquinolone.[1-3§]

MILES Pharmaceutical Division

Miles Inc.
Pharmaceutical Division
400 Morgan Lane
West Haven, CT 06516

the medical aspect of things was discussed, he wanted to chat with me, asked if I had heard from various people, told me that so-and-so has a girlfriend, and I really couldn't deal with that at all.
—Pediatrician, age 34

The pediatrician above spent the rest of her pregnancy in the hospital on tocolytics. As she was waiting it out, counting off the weeks (*Well, now we're at 30—some of them don't get any lung disease at all*), she had to restrict visitors and phone calls because any stress increased the contractions of her uterus. The stress most to be avoided was her mother, and anyone else who might suggest that she had asked for this by working full time as a pediatrician through the first two-thirds of her pregnancy, that she had run a risk and was now paying the consequences.

Anyone who has worked with the parents of babies born prematurely, or babies born with any major problems, knows that the first reaction of many mothers is to blame themselves—and the first reaction of many family members is to blame the mothers. Something you did during this pregnancy made this happen. You worked too hard, you were on your feet too much, you didn't eat right, you washed the floor, you raised your arms up over your head.

There is, in fact, some literature on the pregnancy outcomes of doctors, and it is interesting, both for the data offered and for the different ways those data have been interpreted. Up through 1990, the general feeling in the medical literature was that pregnant physicians had an increased risk of complications. Most of the studies had been done retrospectively, and without control groups; the physicians were compared with the general population, or with a population matched for age and socioeconomic status.

In 1987, Dr. A. Grunebaum and others surveyed 454 obstetricians who had been pregnant and found that those who had been pregnant during residency had a higher than expected rate of intrauterine growth retardation and low-birthweight babies. In 1988, Dr. Nancy H. Miller and colleagues matched physicians with controls for age, race, educational level, parity, and delivery date and found physicians had four times the risk of premature labor and 2.3 times the risk of premature delivery. (These were small studies; the number of physicians actually delivering preterm babies in the Miller study was three.)

In the December 1988 *Western Journal of Medicine,* Dr. Vern L. Katz and colleagues summarized some theories about why physicians might be at increased risk for such complications. Most significant, they suspected, would be the strenuous work schedules of physicians, both during residency and after: "While no association has been found between employment that is not strenuous and adverse pregnancy events, pregnant women with strenuous jobs—excessive work hours, lifting, and being upright for long periods—have been found to be at increased risk for preterm labor, preterm birth, low birth weight, abruptio placentae, toxemia, intrauterine growth retardation, and perinatal mortality. This is the constellation of adverse pregnancy outcomes particular to physicians."

They further developed the pathophysiological argument that these "adverse pregnancy outcomes" might be due to reduced uterine blood flow caused by too much time spent upright as well as by workplace-related stress leading to overproduction of catecholamines and consequent vasoconstriction. They also suggested several other possible mechanisms, including progesterone changes, direct effects on the cervix and uterus from too much standing, and the effects of oxytocin.

An article by Dr. Sharon T. Phelan in *Obstetrics and Gynecology* in 1988 offered a very different picture. Phelan surveyed 1,197 doctors in three specialties—obstetrics and gynecology, psychiatry, and surgery. She collected details on the number of hours worked per week as well as on the complications of pregnancy. Of the 348 women in her survey who had been pregnant during residency, 293 delivered live infants (the other pregnancies ended either in spontaneous or therapeutic abortions). Fifty percent of the 293 said they had had complications. Phelan commented, "Although a complication rate of 50 percent seems to support the belief that residency increases the risk of pregnancy complications, the types of complications varied and the rates were similar to those from the general population." She found no statistically significant differences among the three specialties (although the surgeons and ob-gyns worked longer hours than the psychiatrists). Nor did she find significant differences between the doctors as a group and the general population for any particular complications, except for pregnancy-induced hypertension, which was high, affecting 12 percent of the doctors. Phelan suggested this might be accounted for by a higher maternal age than in the general population.

Dr. Mark A. Klebanoff and colleagues, writing in *The New England Journal of Medicine* in 1990, attempted to overcome some of the problems of the previous studies of pregnancy outcomes among physicians. First, they had a much larger sample: they surveyed 5,079 female residents, 87 percent of whom responded. Second, they had a specific control group: they surveyed the wives of those residents' male colleagues, arguing that these women would be well matched in terms of socioeconomic status, age, and access to medical care. Additionally, the controls would represent a wide variety of occupations, so medicine would be compared with lots of other fields.

They found that 1,293 residents and 1,494 residents' wives became pregnant during the residency period. When the rates of miscarriage, ectopic pregnancy, and stillbirth were compared, there were no significant differences between the female residents and the wives of the male residents. There was, however, a difference in the rate of elective abortion: the female residents were more than three times as likely to terminate their pregnancies (8 percent, versus 2.7 percent). Nine hundred eighty-nine residents and 1,239 residents' wives carried their pregnancies to term. During their pregnancies, the female residents reported working almost double the hours worked by the wives of the male residents. The residents also quit working later (12 days before delivery, as opposed to 35 days before delivery for the wives), and reported significantly less support from co-workers and supervisors.

"Despite major occupational differences," the article concluded, "neither preterm delivery nor delivery of an infant who was small for his or her gestational age was significantly more common among the women residents than among the wives of male residents." On the other hand, when the researchers looked specifically at the group of female residents who reported that they had worked 100 hours or more a week during the third trimester, that group did have an increased risk of preterm delivery compared with the wives of male residents and with the female residents who worked fewer hours. Furthermore, although the female residents did not as a group have more preterm deliveries, they did have a significantly higher rate of preeclampsia and of premature labor that required bed rest or hospitalization.

It is interesting to look at the conclusions drawn from these data, both by the authors themselves and by the *New England Journal* commentary. In the "Discussion" Klebanoff and colleagues wrote, "These findings cast doubt on previously reported associations between employment in physically demanding occupations and an increased risk of adverse pregnancy outcomes. In addition, our results do not support the widely held belief that women residents are at high risk for adverse pregnancy outcomes."

In the same issue, the *Journal* also published a comment on the

Klebanoff article, by Dr. A. Brian Little, which argued that the same limitations on hours that apply to other residents would also be appropriate for pregnant residents. Little concluded that the article had shown that "although all residency programs should now have policies for sensible maternity leave, in fact women are far more like men than George Bernard Shaw recognized."

Four months later the *Journal* published a number of letters about the Klebanoff article, many of them disputing the conclusions that had been drawn. Dr. Jo Ann Rosenfeld of East Tennessee State University wrote, "The question arises whether fetal death, spontaneous abortion, preterm labor, and high blood pressure are the only indicators of difficulty in pregnancy. Are not emotional and marital stress, divorce, lost sleep, poor diet, and difficulty coming to terms with the emotional, financial, and personal issues of pregnancy and early parenthood as important? Is death of the fetus the only outcome worth discussing?"

Another important difference between residents and residents' wives, the letters pointed out, was the rate of elective abortion. Rosenfeld continued: "Isn't it important that there was an increase in the number of voluntary abortions? Doesn't this last figure speak to stress, resentment of co-workers, and overwork as well?" Dr. Heidi D. Nelson of San Francisco General Hospital pointed out that the article had not described the marital status of the female residents—did that have something to do with who chose abortion and who did not? After all, the male residents' wives were, by definition, married. But, in discussing the women who had elected to terminate their pregnancies, Nelson acknowledged that, "The demands of residency and the lack of policy and support were probably factors in many of these decisions."

Overall, the writers felt that the discussion and accompanying commentary minimized the disturbing implications of the data. There seemed to be a suggestion that the authors of the article— if not the *New England Journal* itself—wanted to use these data to show that pregnancy was not a problem for female residents; that remarkably enough they tended to have good outcomes even though, as Klebanoff commented, "It would be difficult to assemble a cohort of women who work longer hours, suffer more sleep deprivation, and are under more stress than residents."

Those who wrote in felt that the problems of pregnancy documented by those same data indicated an urgent need for policy changes, for the recognition of the special needs of pregnant physicians—a recognition that the *Journal* had somehow denied when it titled the commentary, "Why Can't a Woman Be More Like a Man?" and concluded that, in fact, she can.

As women become more of a presence in medicine, it may be that assumptions will change and that instead of repeating over and over, "Don't worry, we can do it, no special favors," we will be able to look at pregnant physicians and think about what is best for them and for their babies. As Dr. Nancy H. Miller and Dr. Vern L. Katz, writing together in the *New England Journal*, stated, "It is ironic that we, the medical community, feel compelled to document whether objective untoward outcomes occur with pregnancies during residency. Prudent obstetricians would not advise their pregnant patients to work 80 to 100 hours per week, for 24 or more hours per shift, under stressful conditions."

CHAPTER THREE

YOUR PATIENTS, YOUR CHILDREN

ne thing the practice of medicine has in common with the parental care of babies and young children is the opportunity for an unwonted (and unwanted) familiarity with the bodily fluids of others. This was brought home to me most vividly when my son was a few months old and I was in the early part of my third-year-student internal medicine rotation at one of our nation's more distinguished and self-satisfied teaching hospitals. It was my first clinical rotation; I was profoundly unsure of myself and rapidly coming to the conclusion that I didn't much care for internal medicine. Everyone else—other students, interns, attendings—seemed to know so much. They seemed to thrive on rapid-fire medical give-and-take.

I tried hard to style myself as the sensitive one, the one who really cared about the patients. But in hindsight I think the truth is that I was miserably aware of my own lackluster performance, and miserably aware that I had trouble making myself care about the patients. I was astonished by how much hospital-based internal medicine seemed to consist of treating very elderly and debilitated nursing-home patients who were brought in by ambulance because they had stopped making urine, or had had fever for several weeks, or had passed a bloody stool. I watched the house staff put these patients through one test after another, and felt sorry for the patients, sorry for the house staff, but most of all, sorry for myself. This was not what I had expected medicine to be like: constant remarks on rounds like, "Well, there may be some interesting pathology here, but there's not going to be anything we can do about it."

One day one of the interns asked me if I would come help him disimpact Mr. B., an 80-odd-year-old nursing-home resident who had not spoken for some years. Mr. B. had been bedbound for many months and had developed overwhelming constipation that was causing him terrible pain and threatening him with perforation. Laxatives had failed and enemas had failed. The intern rolled Mr. B. into the fetal position, and I disimpacted him manually, a task I found disgusting, of course, but peculiarly satisfying. If it was in some ways the perfect metaphor for the experience of being a third-year medical student, it was also a task I understood and could complete properly. I thought I might be able to leave Mr. B. more comfortable than I had found him.

To take my mind off the details of the process, I allowed myself some lofty reflections on how the end of life is like the beginning of life. I thought of how I spent my time at home attending to Benjamin's diapers, inspecting the consistency of his little poops. Now here I was trying to be gentle with a man eight decades older, just as dependent, and just as unable to communicate.

The intern, perhaps feeling a little apologetic for having made the medical student carry out this singularly unappealing procedure, said to me, "Well, this is what being a doctor is like sometimes."

"It's a lot like being a mother," I said, continuing to dig around in Mr. B.'s rectum.

The intern smiled at me, and told me I had a good attitude and would go far. I remember that partly because words of praise in that particular clerkship were few and far between for me. But I also remember it because it was true that after a few months of motherhood, I seemed to have lost much of my squeamishness. I'm not talking about the heroic victory that some medical students have to win over themselves in order to help out in surgery; I had never been terribly upset by blood and operations. I'm talking about reluctance to come into close contact with the excrement or vomit of others, the literal reluctance to get my hands dirty. I had felt some of it even before Benjamin was born, thinking with distaste about dirty diapers and wondering how one was supposed to deal with them. Of course, after the first time you find yourself up to your wrists in your child's dirty diaper, the whole thing begins to seem like a necessary though unpleasant part of life. No one with an infant can afford to be truly fussy.

Medical training also left me with different standards for what is mentionable and what is not, for what is disgusting and what is merely real. When my son was 5 and I was hugely and publicly pregnant with my daughter, he started to quiz me one day in the supermarket. I had gone over the mechanics of conception, pregnancy, and childbirth, not so much as a doctor but as a forward-thinking, liberal parent. I had read him the proper books and shown him the proper diagrams. And then one day in the supermarket:

Him [*at the top of his lungs*]: Mom! After the baby comes out of you?"

Me [*lowered voice, self-conscious in my rotundity*]: Yes?

Him [*even louder*]: When they cut the cord?

Me: Yes?

Him: Do they cut the end that's near you or the end that's near the baby?

Well, even though I was convinced that every single person in the supermarket was listening and picturing me in childbirth, I couldn't help being proud of him. Such an advanced question! Didn't it indicate a real appreciation of anatomy and physiology? Didn't it suggest he had really been giving some thought to the specifics of umbilical cords and vaginal delivery?

Me [*softly but clearly*]: The end that's near the baby.

Him [*louder than ever, amazed*]: So then you just have this cord hanging out of you, Mom?

I imagined every single other shopper picturing the scene: me with the bloody cord hanging between my legs. It was not really the moment I would have chosen to explain about the placenta, but I did my best, and Benjamin listened with close attention. As I self-consciously paid for my groceries, I reflected on how for me these bloody images usually held no particular power to shock. But because they obviously referred to me in my unmistakably pregnant state, and because we were in a supermarket, not a hospital, I heard them all differently. I imagined how they would sound to normal people, and I was embarrassed.

Most of the time, though, I have enjoyed showing my son how his body works, even looking up diagrams in my medical textbooks with him. I have an anatomy coloring book of which he is particularly fond (it's what got me through gross anatomy); he has told me approvingly that I am pretty good at coloring inside the lines.

If pregnancy is a lesson in being a patient, in feeling your body out of your own control and in looking to doctors and nurses for advice and for answers, then life with an infant is a lesson in responsibility. The knowledge that this small and completely defenseless body is yours to protect, that there is never any signing out, never any real cross-coverage, is one of the most overwhelming messages of parenthood. No one feels ready for it; no one feels confident. All the advice books in the world do not leave you feeling prepared; they may only serve as reminders that there are rights and wrongs, disasters to be avoided and good outcomes to be courted. The analogy to medical training is fairly blatant.

I had my two children during my training. The entire model of clinical training, both for students and for residents, involves perpetually ascending stakes. It's the "see one, do one, teach one" inflationary spiral of residency: as soon as you're comfortable with one level of responsibility, they up the ante and you find yourself off-balance again, wondering if you can cope at this new level. I remember my first night on call as an intern, realizing that most of the other doctors were actually going to go home and leave me in the NICU with all those sick babies. Was it possible we would all get through the night? And I remember myself as a senior resident, realizing that everyone was going to go home and leave me with a bunch of sick babies—and with an intern to supervise. The basic medical injunction to do no harm, the terror of the doctor-in-training praying to get through the night without hurting anyone, the frightened awe of the new parent watching a sleeping baby and thinking inchoate and unvoiced prayers for health and safety and a good, long life—for me, these overlap and flicker in and out of focus when I think about that part of my life.

Doctors who have their children a little further down the line are already used to a burden of responsibility for the lives of others. A baby to care for brings the new wrinkle of helpless, unreasoning affection. In medicine, you learn or absorb various techniques to keep your emotional distance from your patients. You learn the uses of humor and professional jargon, and you learn ways to deal with decisions that don't turn out well or are out-and-out mistakes. Many of these coping mechanisms are healthy, others less so, but some such mechanism is necessary. You could not go on in medicine if you grieved for each patient's pain or problem as you would for that of a family member. You can take responsibility, offer help, offer judgments about what is or is not likely to help, but you must protect yourself, keep yourself intact.

With a new baby, you can't protect yourself at all. You feel some version of that same intense responsibility, but now it is mixed with total protectiveness, total affection, and the blurring of boundaries that takes place when your life opens up to include a child. No parent watches a baby in pain without wishing to take over that pain:

I'd do the teething for you if I could; I'd suffer the immunizations if it meant you didn't have to.

Medical training is a process of instilling heavy responsibility while helping those who assume it to keep boundaries between themselves and those they are caring for. Interestingly, there is a great deal of overlap with the specifics of parental authority. Both doctors and parents are expected to understand issues of physical safety, to field complaints of wildly varying intensity and decide what is serious and what is not. Both must assume some larger moral authority over the body.

In the past, the jobs of mother and physician were seen as mutually exclusive. Although there were female doctors in the 19th century, the assumption made (at least by many who wrote about them) was that these women had chosen medicine instead of marriage and motherhood, and that the two choices had to be mutually exclusive because they had so much in common. In Sarah Orne Jewett's fascinating 1884 novel, *A Country Doctor*, the heroine, Nan Prince, must choose between marriage and family and the career she wants as a physician. Her guardian and mentor, old Dr. Leslie, reflects upon the choice: "He tried to assure himself that while a man's life is strengthened by his domestic happiness, a woman's must either surrender itself wholly, or relinquish entirely the claims of such duties, if she would achieve distinction or satisfaction elsewhere. The two cannot be taken together in a woman's life as in a man's. One must be made of lesser consequence, though the very natures of both domestic and professional life need all the strength which can be brought to them." For many doctors nowadays, male and female (but especially female), life is a struggle to do what Dr. Leslie thought could not be done.

There are times when I look to my children to provide me with spiritual succor, to offer me images of health and joy. Recently I drove straight from the funeral of a 14-month-old patient to my daughter's day-care center, hurrying more than usual because I wanted to see her, vigorous and surrounded by vigorous children, to balance out the image of the small body in the coffin.

There are also, to be perfectly honest, plenty of times when work offers a refuge from the vagaries of child-rearing and family life. A young internist who moonlights frequently to supplement his family income told a story of being on call one weekend when his year-old daughter had a high fever and an ear infection. He described his guilty relief that he was not at home helping to cope with a sick baby whose misery would make him miserable, and the ways he tried to make up for his absence when he did go home. I recognized the syndrome; I too have found myself in the hospital overnight when one of my children was sick at home. There is relief at not having to watch your child suffer, at having an ironclad excuse—you can't be there, you're at work saving lives. And then there is guilt for having felt that relief, and knowing your partner suspects it.

There are ways in which medical moments seem like funhouse-mirror images of parental experiences. And I'm not just talking about disimpacting an elderly man. When I think about night wakenings, for example, I conjure images of myself as an intern, asleep in scrubs on a folding cot in the conference room, the beeper going off, the nurse knocking on the door, me shuffling to my feet and padding down the hall to watch a child's respirations, draw antibiotic levels, do a sepsis workup. But I also think about the nights at home, the hesitant baby cries from the basket across the room, the period of lying still and pretending not to hear them, of waiting to see if maybe Larry will give in first and get up. And I think about the unbelievable, exhausted sweetness of those middle-of-the-night encounters with my own children, nursing in the rocking chair, falling asleep beside them on my bed. These images blur—responding to my patients, responding to my children, the weariness, the middle-of-the-night feeling, the strangeness of those years of always being tired.

Back when I was doing internal medicine, I had this stupid joke all worked out about how it was actually an advantage to be a third-year medical student with an infant because of all that practice you get in waking up at night. *The only problem is,* I thought I could say, *the nurse wakes me up and I go and diaper the patient.* But the truth was that it worked the other way. In the hospital, I always woke knowing exactly where I was and what I had to be worrying about—I suppose because, in the hospital, I was always sufficiently worried that I never really slept soundly. At home, however, I would let myself go and sleep deeply, and when the baby's cries woke me I would often find myself unsure, panicked for at least a split second by the idea that I was in the hospital and something was happening but I didn't know what, that I had dropped the threads.

All through the night and all through the day, doctors respond to events in the lives of patients. When doctors' partners and children talk about life in a physician's family, one common theme is their awareness of emergencies, those summonses that drag Daddy or Mommy out of the house, away from the table, that conflict with the school play or the promised picnic. Ironically, a parent's job also involves constant availability, constant readiness to face crises large and small. This is what can give you that pulled-at feeling, that sense that everywhere you look, at home and at work, there are people who need you and need your help.

Dr. David Hilfiker, in his moving book *Healing the Wounds*, tells the story of an unsuccessful resuscitation in a patient with colon cancer, Charles, who suddenly dies. "When I arrive home, my emotions are a tangled web. Laurel, my oldest daughter, wants to show me her Sunday school project, but I can barely muster the patience. I go outside and begin to work on the woodpile. . . . The physical exertion begins to bring the parts of my soul together again. Only then does the nagging doubt begin. Should I have terminated the CPR so quickly on Charles? Was there anything else we could have done to resuscitate him?"

Just as in medicine we are dependent on the people who cover for us and who back us up, as parents we are dependent on the people who help take care of our children. Dr. Marjorie A. Bowman and Dr. Deborah I. Allan, in their book *Stress and Women Physicians* (1985), devote much of the chapter on child-rearing to the issue of choosing a mode of child care. Physician parents have many of the same requirements as other busy parents; everyone wants responsible caretakers, flexible hours, and a bright, happy, stimulating environment. Bowman and Allan have no hesitation in calling child care "perhaps the biggest bane of the woman physician mother's existence." They cite a 1983 survey that considered how such doctors arranged for child care. The survey found that 18 percent had live-in au pairs and 29 percent used babysitters who came to their homes. Only 20 percent used day-care centers, and another 20 percent used other forms of child care outside the home.

A 1989 study by Dr. Sara Sinal and colleagues found that the most satisfactory form of child care for this group was the au pair or babysitter at home. It is not difficult to understand why doctors would have this preference. This kind of child care usually allows the most flexibility and does away with the frantic morning rush of getting children dressed, out the door, and off to day care. As a day-care mother myself, I can understand how daunting the rigid schedules of a day-care center can seem to people whose jobs reliably keep them later than scheduled and reliably interrupt their homeward dashes with beepers, curbside consultations, and sudden emergencies.

At my particular day-care center, we have an institution called the late-parent room, where children are taken by the teachers when their parents have not arrived to pick them up by the appointed time. Parents take turns staffing the late-parent room, waiting with the kids for the arrival of the late parents. My own daughter, at age 2, is deeply attached to the late-parent room, having spent so many pleasant moments there while her mother drove dangerously through rush hour traffic, attempting to complete a 32-minute drive in 25 minutes or less. In fact, my daughter has come to love the late-parent room, where other parents—no doubt pitying her semiorphan state—read aloud to her and play games with her. If I arrive on time, as does occasionally happen, she begins to demand to go to the late-parent room, and when I try to stuff her into her coat and take her home, she begins to wail.

The other tremendous disadvantage of day care is of course that your children can't go when they're sick. Now, if you happen to be a physician, and unscrupulous to boot, you can try dosing them with Tylenol (or Dimetapp, or Robitussin) and sneaking them in, assuring the teachers with the full weight of professional training in your voice that the child has a little sniffle but that's all—nothing serious, certainly nothing worth staying home for. (Naturally, I would never do such a thing; the very idea shocks me to the core of my being.)

Still, I love day care. I love watching my kids move through a structure that stays steady from year to year so that each fall they move up a room and graduate to bigger-kid status. I love watching them make friends, and watching them take possession; at 2, my daughter knows that the day-care center is her place, where she knows the rules and the routines. And while I don't particularly love it when she gets sick and has to stay home, I remind myself that I'd rather stay home to be with her because she's sick than stay home to care for her because the babysitter's sick.

But I have no trouble understanding why many doctors prefer in-home help for taking care of small children. In fact, up until quite recently, in-home help was the sine qua non for the doctor's household. It was, of course, provided by a full-time, live-in doctor's wife. Perhaps one reason that many doctors, both male and female, find themselves wanting an au pair is a sense that a person who's in medicine ought to have a full-time domestic caretaker, that a career in medicine requires that kind of support, and if neither partner is able (or willing) to provide it, then someone must be hired. *Hippocrates' Handmaidens* by Esther Nitzberg, published in 1991, is a study of women married to physicians. It has a thorough index, but "child care" is not one of the categories listed (nor is "day care," or "babysitter"). By and large the women profiled in this book are in charge of the care of their children, without, it would seem, too much help from their doctor husbands. The chapter about doctors as fathers is entitled, "Kids, Who Remembers the Color of Your Father's Eyes?"

Arrowsmith, the 1925 Sinclair Lewis novel that has helped lure many an idealist into medicine and medical research, offers an interesting if discouraging perspective on the dedicated physician as parent. Martin Arrowsmith's son, John, is born at the end of the book, when Martin has married his second wife, the rich and socially well-connected Joyce, who does not understand the intellectual fervor that drives him in his research. Joyce's labor is covered in a couple of sentences. She suffers horribly: "She was grotesquely stretched on a chair of torture and indignity. . . . Her face was green with agony." But the child himself does not inspire love or protection from his father: "John Arrowsmith was straight of back and straight of limb—ten good pounds he had weighed at birth— and he was gay of eye when he had ceased to be a raw wrinkled grub and become a man-child. Joyce worshiped him, and Martin was afraid of him, because he saw that this minuscule aristocrat, this child born to the self-approval of riches, would some day condescend to him." And in fact, when Martin ultimately leaves worldly things (including his wife) far behind him, setting off into the wilderness to pursue scientific truths in a spectacularly sentimental and nonsensical conclusion to what is otherwise an extremely realistic novel, he leaves his son behind with scarcely a second thought. The child is nothing but a drag, a distraction, a tie to what he must escape.

It is interesting to note that Lewis was the son, grandson, nephew, and brother of doctors. He put into his novel much of the detail he knew of doctors' lives and much of the respect he felt for medical lives, for scientific dedication and the devotion to advancing medical understanding and public health. But Martin Arrowsmith's abandonment of his son is tossed off in a paragraph; the author clearly does not feel that it in any way undermines the heroic stature of his protagonist. (You can't help imagining how it would figure if the doctor in question were female!)

Boris Pasternak's *Doctor Zhivago,* which appeared in 1958, features an even more famous literary man of medicine than Arrowsmith. Zhivago, too, was a father. He was separated from his children not by his medical career but by the whirlwind of revolution. The children are not important characters in the epic novel, and Zhivago only occasionally thinks of them—far less than he thinks of Lara. Far away in Siberia, Zhivago reflects upon himself as a father: "He is away, he has always been away, all his life he has remained apart from them. What kind of father is he? Is it possible for a real father always to be away?" Some would say that such sentiments could be attributed to doctors in middle-class America as well as in revolutionary Russia.

There is no great literary tradition of doctors who are also fathers, no easy pantheon of images in which the healer and the parent overlap. In George Eliot's novel *Middlemarch*, Dr. Lydgate, one of the most famous and most sensitively drawn physicians in 19th-century literature, loses his baby before it is born. His lovely but disobedient wife, Rosamond, goes horseback riding during the pregnancy, and the horse takes fright at the crash of a falling tree, in turn frightening her. She loses the baby she is carrying, and in the total self-absorption that makes her such a monster, she refuses to acknowledge that she is at fault: "In all future conversations on the subject, Rosamond was mildly certain that the ride had made no difference, and that if she had stayed at home the same symptoms would have come on and would have ended in the same way, because she had felt something like them before."

One literary physician who is involved in raising his own child is Sloan Crockett in *The Group*, Mary McCarthy's scandalous 1963 bestseller about eight women who graduate from Vassar in 1933. One of them, Priss Hartshorn, marries Sloan, a forward-thinking young pediatrician. As soon as their child, Stephen, is born, Sloan takes the opportunity to put into effect the most modern theories of child-rearing. To Priss's mother's horror, those theories involve a return to what she thinks of as the Dark Ages—that is, Priss is going to nurse her own baby rather than allow him to be bottle-fed. Priss's mother and the nurses at New York Hospital are not at all convinced by the pediatrician's newfangled talk about immunities and the benefits of breastfeeding on a rigorously regulated schedule. And the pediatrician is not impressed by the nurses' reports that the baby, rendered hungry by the rigors of the schedule, cries for hours every night; as long as the weight curve is rising, Sloan asserts, the baby is getting enough to eat.

"Lying in bed tensely listening to Stephen's mournful cry," McCarthy writes, "Priss suddenly did not understand why Sloan was so strong for breast-feeding. Was it entirely for the reasons he gave—

the medical reasons? . . . It crossed her mind that Sloan, who was just starting in practice, might regard her nursing Stephen as a sort of advertisement. He liked to make a point of his differences with dear old Dr. Drysdale, who had taken him into his office and who had practically introduced the bottle into New York society. . . . Her pride was deflated by the thought that Sloan was using her to prove his theories, like a testimonial in a magazine." Every doctor who has been a parent, and every doctor's spouse, will know immediately that Priss has hit on something important in her terrible suspicion. It is impossible for a physician not to feel, however faintly, the pressure of performing as a parent and maintaining the current medical standard of child-rearing.

To the eyes of a 1990s pediatrician, of course, Sloan is entirely correct about breastfeeding (though foolish in his insistence on a schedule while the baby is crying). Still, he is presented as somewhat distant from his own wife and child, unable to understand the implications of his dicta even so close to home. He has science on his side, but he has never actually cared for a child. Priss believes her husband is a deeply compassionate man, but that he has had to develop a brusque façade, an armor, because of all the suffering he sees. Still, "it struck her as peculiar that nurses, who heard more crying than doctors did, did not develop an armor against it."

It will be left to Priss to carry out her husband's theories, and left to their child to thwart them, and in so doing reproach Priss with her failure as a woman, a mother, and a pediatrician's wife. She knows she ought to have a showpiece child, a child in whom proper methods produce proper results, and that any lapses will be laid at her door. Her husband may set policy, but he is not about to care for his own child from one day to the next.

In fact, the male physician left (usually widowed) to care for his own child is an interesting figure both in literature and in history. Consider Dr. Gibson, the country doctor in Elizabeth Gaskell's 1864 novel *Wives and Daughters*, and his daughter, Molly. "He was a widower, and likely to remain so; his domestic affections were centered on little Molly, but even to her, in their most private moments, he did not give way to much expression of his feelings; his most caressing appellation for her was 'Goosey,' and he took a pleasure in bewildering her infant mind with his badinage. He had rather a contempt for demonstrative people, arising from his medical insight into the consequences to health of uncontrolled feeling." Thus Gaskell suggests that a doctor may at best be an unsentimental parent.

A fascinating combination of conventional and controversial attitudes, she rejected 19th-century prejudices and boldly pursued her desire to study medicine.

Miles is proud to present this series on...

Powerful Innovators

Powerful Physician

Elizabeth Blackwell (1821-1910)

The same young woman who worried that she would never learn to dance gracefully became one of this country's most humanitarian doctors. Twenty-eight medical schools rejected her before she was accepted by New York State's Geneva College, from which she graduated in 1849.

Despite the loss of an eye to disease, Blackwell started a general practice in New York in 1851. Six years later, together with her sister, she opened a clinic for poor women and tirelessly fought for improvements in her patients' living and working conditions. Her battles for good health care continued as she opened the first visiting-nurse service in the United States, managed the Union's nursing corps during the Civil War, and founded the Women's Medical College of the New York Infirmary.

Blackwell's courage and determination made it possible for thousands of women to earn medical degrees by the time of her death in 1910.

Powerful Antimicrobial

Rapid, bactericidal power—that's what you get from intravenous ciprofloxacin, which has demonstrated, in vitro, complete killing of an isolate of Pseudomonas aeruginosa *in 2 hours...faster than any other leading antimicrobial.* Ciprofloxacin has also demonstrated excellent serum concentration and tissue penetration.[†]*

Cipro® I.V.
(ciprofloxacin)

The most potent fluoroquinolone.[1-3]*

Powerful Numbers

speak for themselves:

4 ... *The number of stages of cell growth during which ciprofloxacin actively kills— the lag, exponential growth, stationary, and dying-off phases.**

6.2 ... *The number of times higher ciprofloxacin bronchial tissue concentration is than its serum levels, at 1 hour.*†‡*

96 ... *The percent susceptibility of 71,389 clinical isolates of Enterobacteriaceae to ciprofloxacin.**

The most potent fluoroquinolone.[1-3]*

See complete prescribing information at the end of this book.

In vitro activity does not necessarily imply a correlation with *in vivo* results.
†Tissue/fluid penetration is regarded as essential to therapeutic efficacy, but penetration levels have not been correlated with specific therapeutic results.
‡Penetration levels are calculated from mean serum and tissue values.

Miles Inc.
Pharmaceutical Division
400 Morgan Lane
West Haven, CT 06516

There is also the historical case of the Scottish widower Dr. James Loftus Marsden, who in 1852 hired a French governess, Célestine Doudet, to care for his five daughters while he pursued his medical career. Mary Hartman has written about this fascinating case in *Victorian Murderesses*, for Célestine Doudet abused the girls in her care so brutally that one of them eventually died. The ironic twist to the case was that the governess's abusive regime was partly prescribed by the good doctor himself, who in accordance with Victorian medical wisdom was determined to go to any lengths to prevent his daughters from masturbating. We thus see in this strange and awful 19th-century murder case the doctor as parent, the doctor as consumer of child care, and the doctor as expert, attempting to bring his own ideas of scientific child-rearing to bear on his own daughters.

When Sigmund Freud in 1911 analyzed the case of Daniel Paul Schreber, who suffered bizarre delusions of torture at the hands of "soul-murderers," he attributed the case to paranoia and to the Oedipus complex. Freud did not pick up on the fact that Schreber was the son of a well-known 19th-century German doctor, an expert on child-rearing who had devised a disciplinary regime for his own child so sadistically rigorous that today we would call it child abuse. The doctor as expert can be dangerous to his children.

Elizabeth Gaskell allowed her character, Dr. Gibson, a happier relationship with his daughter. Although he bewildered Molly and refused to give way to anything demonstrative, "the child grew to understand her father well," and the two enjoyed a pleasant relationship of "half banter, half seriousness, but altogether confidential friendship." The doctor as parent, by Victorian standards, was not quite parental. The combination of "half banter, half seriousness," which here characterized the relations between parent and child, would certainly call to mind for doctors and patients today the formula for bedside manner.

CHAPTER FOUR

WHEN THEY GET SICK

I'm very demanding of my own pediatrician. As a parent, I want to be seen when I want to be seen; I don't want to wait. I don't ever examine my own children, but I don't bring my baby in on a whim, either. I assess how toxic my child is, and when I do come in, I give a complete history—he has a very good patient, but I demand a lot. For example, I called him yesterday and said my 2-year-old needed to be seen. I wouldn't accept him saying no.

Your life experience molds who you are and how you react. When I was a resident, we had a mobile ICU that picked up sick newborn babies from outlying rural areas. You would go out, as a resident, and at least let the mother see and touch the baby before you carried it away in the ICU. I understood on an intellectual level, but after I had children, the thought of being that mother and having that child taken away—I understood all the frustration, anxiety, vulnerability, fears. It's different when it's your kid lying there.

I feel I'm a much better pediatrician for having children. That's what it took for me.

—Pediatrician, age 42

hildren's illnesses mark every parent. Even for the fortunate parents whose children never know anything more than routine sore throats and runny noses, those days and nights when a child is less than healthy stay in the memory; everything you most worry about is there in shadow. But for most of us, more frightening memories are accumulated in the standard rush through childhood.

When my son, Benjamin, was 4, he fractured his femur when he fell down the porch steps one morning as he and Larry were heading out for day care. I was a junior resident, getting ready to leave the hospital when Larry called me to say Benjamin wouldn't stop crying. I came driving home (post-call, sleep-deprived, and dangerous) as fast as I could, and held him on my lap as Larry drove us back to the same hospital. I remember everything about that morning, of course. I remember Benjamin in the CT scan, when they were looking for internal injuries. I remember telling him an endless story—all swordplay and heroics—to help him stay calm. I remember making a big fuss about which anesthesiologist would take care of Benjamin when he went to the OR to have a pin put in his knee (I wanted to be sure someone I knew and trusted would be in charge of my child's airway). And I remember my son's face, that day of his sudden, harsh acquaintance with pain.

The orthopedic residents wrote their standard pain-control measures for Benjamin: he could have IM morphine, PRN. What this turned out to mean was that when his leg hurt, he would cry; the nurse would come and give him a shot; he'd cry harder because of the shot; and just as he began to calm down, his leg would begin to hurt again. I demanded that the nurses page the orthopedic resident at 1 a.m., and I furiously demanded IV morphine for Benjamin. I assured the resident that I had given IV morphine many times, that I had managed morphine drips, for heaven's sake. I could hear in my mind how that orthopedist was going to quote me on morning rounds, how he would exaggerate the authority I claimed for myself, how I was not the kind of mother a doctor wants to deal with.

As for my daughter, Josephine—well, how about the time she aspirated the chicken and macaroni and started to turn blue, and had to be pulled out of the high chair and banged on? Will I ever forget what it was like watching my own daughter get fluoroscoped—watching her heart beat inside her ribs and thinking with confusion about what I knew about systole and diastole. I was watching my little girl's heart, pumping blood to her body and brain, keeping her alive.

As a pediatrician, it's an admission of your own shortcomings if you can't take care of your children. I came to grips with this by making the decision that I would never take care of my own children; I would relinquish the role of physician and become mother. When I'm in a doctor's office, I am very much the mother, and that was a conscious decision. If the doctor says, "I don't need to tell you this," I say, "I'm the mother here."

On the other hand, as a parent, common things didn't frighten me. I was relatively calm. Even when my daughter had her face smashed in this weekend, I definitely took on my professional role: Let's get things done and get them done right. There was only one time I really lost control. My daughter fell off the changer. I couldn't catch her—I really got upset.

—Pediatrician, age 42

When doctors speak about their experiences as parents, one theme that comes through again and again is the confusion of roles when their children get sick. Even with minor illnesses, there are special tensions. When a doctor's child gets sick, does the doctor diagnose and treat? There are doctors who do almost all the health care for their own children, though this seems to have been more common a generation ago. And there are also doctors who are so concerned that the roles be kept separate they are reluctant even to look at a sore throat with a flashlight—something that my mother, with no medical training whatsoever, considered a parental prerogative.

Most of us are probably somewhere in the middle. I actually do check my own children's ears when they get colds and fevers; this is left over from my first child, who had many, many ear infections before the age of 2. The pediatrician we went to at the time kept telling me that I had to remember I was the mother, not the doctor. But when it came to a question of whether to drag my miserable baby out on a cold, snowy night to sit in an emergency room or to check his ears and give him a dose of amoxicillin if necessary, I had no trouble choosing. The pediatrician we go to now seems to expect this as a matter of course; when I call to report that my daughter is sick, he asks me whether I've checked her ears.

Recently I thought she might be developing an otitis (though it was a pretty soft call) and I administered the first dose of amoxicillin. My daughter, who has never willingly swallowed a dose of medicine in her entire life, did her usual fountain act, spurting forth a spume of pink, frothy spit, then screaming her protest at the indignities being forced upon her (otoscopes! amoxicillin!). I cleaned up, reflecting as usual on how strange it is that some people consider the ear exam an especially traumatic experience for a child, as if it violates the parent-child bond in some terrible way. Personally, I would rather check my daughter's ears than give her medicine. For that matter, I think, I would rather draw her blood than give her medicine (and there have been moments in her fierce little life when I have thought that performing a full sepsis workup on her would have been less traumatic for us both than washing her hair, but never mind that).

Anyway, being less than fully convinced that my daughter really did have otitis, I was reluctant to keep giving her medicine. So I took her to the pediatrician. When he looked in her ear, he found that his otoscope was blocked—her ear canals were full of amoxicillin. I held her down, he cleaned it out, and when he got a good look, he decided that her tympanic membranes were normal.

> *My second kid has been a lot sicker than my first. I can deal with them being sick; I'm not one of those people who developed symptoms in medical school. I can deal with their illnesses better than my wife can. But it's been harder with the second one. She had GI problems, and we embarked on a mega-workup. Upper GI, upper and lower endoscopies—it was the worst day of my life. To see that little face with tears in her eyes looking up at you like you're supposed to get her out of this—it was incredibly wrenching.*
> —Internist, age 33

For pediatricians, the connections between what you live through with your own children and how you handle your patients are obvious. No one who has lived through colic will ever underestimate the agonies of parents with a colicky baby. Once you've made the jump yourself—hand on your own infant's forehead—you understand how other parents leap quickly from a feverish baby to the fear of a very sick baby, to images of meningitis, of a brain that is cooking inside a feverish head. But as a physician, you feel a responsibility to be more rational than other parents, and sometimes you go overboard in the wrong direction.

Dr. Jeffrey Avner wrote in *Pediatrics* in 1991 about his reaction to his daughter's severe case of croup. His wife took the baby into the bathroom and turned on the shower. ("During my pediatric residency I had given many of my clinic patients' parents the same advice.") The baby did not improve very much, but he decided not to take her to the hospital. "If she had been someone else's child I would have admitted her," he acknowledged. "Perhaps I was afraid her condition would improve after the drive to the emergency room and my fellow residents would think I was overreacting. You would think doctors would be more attuned to the dangers of their children's illnesses, yet, all too often, we wait too long."

The baby was admitted to the hospital the next day, treated with racemic epinephrine, and transferred to the ICU. A pediatrician who watches his or her own child go through something like that inevitably feels caught in some cruel irony of life. You know so much—all the language, the purpose of each therapy. And unfortunately, you know all the possible bad outcomes. Avner wrote: "I took a few deep breaths and entered the 'treatment room.' There was my daughter with a blank stare on her face from the exhaustion of putting everything she had into each breath. I was trying to be strong, maybe by removing part of my emotion as I had done with some patients to whom I had grown too close. But this was my daughter; I, her father, had no answers or power to help her. I turned and left the room almost immediately. How I wished I were the doctor and not the parent."

No one knows better than doctors the limits of what modern medicine can accomplish in sparing pain and in curing illness. And nothing dramatizes those limits more than the experience of having your own child in the treatment room. Avner's daughter recovered, and he was left, he concludes, with a very different understanding of what the parents of his patients are feeling.

Pediatricians are forced through their work to learn over and over the harsh lesson of vulnerability. Yes, most kids are healthy. Yes, most pediatric illnesses are brief and benign, and even kids who get very sick usually recover (compared with adults, they recover fast). Yes, we live in a time (and a place) when most children will live to grow up because the standard scourges of childhood have been largely defeated by sanitation, immunization, and preventive care. But if you practice pediatrics you still see the other children, the ones who fall through all the safety nets.

> I walked through the ER and saw a kid my son's age who was stung by a bee and had a respiratory arrest; it made me feel sick. I rely on pure denial: that stuff only happens in the hospital, and I live 30 miles out. I use that drive home as decompression time.
>
> —Pediatrician, age 42

In order to deal day in and day out with the problems of the human body, many doctors build imaginary barriers. But no matter what bargains you make with fate, no matter what defenses you put up, everyone who works with children and has children at home is prey to certain moments when those defenses fall. Last summer a previously healthy 2-year-old was brought into the intensive care unit. He had choked on a grape, and by the time the EMTs arrived he was essentially flat-line. They resuscitated him and brought him in for the agonizing medical and ethical deliberations that go into decision-making in the case of a 2-year-old with brain death. The EMTs offered a description—passed along in the hospital—of how the grape had been wedged into the trachea like a ball in a socket. That night the nurses in the ICU took turns calling home. They told their husbands, their babysitters, "Throw out all the grapes. Don't let the kids have any grapes." In my house, we outlawed grapes for the rest of the summer. At my day-care center, I made a long, impassioned speech to the teachers about the importance of cutting grapes up before giving them to the children.

You need to tell yourself that the things you see happen to your patients will not happen to you or to those you love most. Even in pediatrics, when you think of your own child you keep up those distinctions. *This could not happen to my child,* you say to yourself, *because I am careful about poisons. Because his immunizations are up to date. Because I would never let him get this sick without taking him to a doctor. Because I say it will not.* Then something as random as a grape breaches the wall; accidents happen. Your child is vulnerable, and all your skill does not offer you any guarantees.

An anonymous "pediatrician mother," also writing in *Pediatrics,* described the process of coming to suspect that her 4-year-old daughter had been sexually abused by her father, the writer's ex-husband. Again, the writer strikes the note of someone who knows too much, someone who knows the vocabulary that will be applied to her own child. "When her perineum was redder and more irritated than I had ever seen in my five years of practice and there were two superficial abrasions between her vagina and anus, I even managed to hide my shaking," she wrote. As in Avner's story, however, the knowledge was mixed with denial. "The bleeding abrasions on her perineum caused me to be more afraid than I ever had been before, but when a phone call told me that her pediatrician was asleep for the night, my need for denial allowed me to drop the matter until the next morning."

The writer concluded, once again, that her daughter's pain may have made her a more sensitive physician, that the pain may have meaning for some future child who comes to her for help and finds someone who understands. (She also pleaded with pediatricians to remember that sexual abuse occurs in physician families, and other families of high social status.)

Through our children's illnesses, we are plunged into a complex matrix of caring, caretaking, worrying, and grieving. If we can allow ourselves to acknowledge the ambiguities of the situation, we may end up with a better understanding of the uses of authority, denial, prayer, and plain old unreasoning love.

On the other hand, it is often very difficult for doctors to tolerate such ambiguity right there within the borders of the family. Esther Nitzberg, in *Hippocrates' Handmaidens*, tells a story about her 24-year-old son being diagnosed with ulcerative colitis. After first denying his symptoms, the son, Mitch, finally discussed the problem with his father, an internist. From there the family progressed to a specialist, who did the full workup. Nitzberg writes of her horror when the specialist, by way of explaining the diagnosis to Mitch, concentrated on the worst possible outcomes. "You will probably not have to be hospitalized or probably won't need a colostomy," he said. He then asked the family if they had any questions.

"To my astonishment, my husband, Jerry the doctor, was stone silent," writes Nitzberg. "My savior, Mitch's protector, our connection to God when it comes to our health care, spoke not a word. Just sitting there, I thought at the time, he's colluding with the specialist to keep us in the dark.

"Later I realized Jerry could not deal with the diagnosis. He was totally denying the fact of his son's illness and future with a chronic disease. We were all devastated and so into our own selfish responses that Mitch, who is so reserved anyway, was almost overlooked in the picture. . . . We learned that no one understands the cause of the illness and there is no cure—from the book, I might add; no information was forthcoming from the physician, either specialist or father-doctor. Silence, brooding, and noncommunication were the modus operandi."

It is a very heavy load to expect someone to be at one and the same time a stricken father (or mother) and also a savior, protector, connection to God.

When a family member is sick, many physicians find some comfort in retreating into their professional demeanor. You think about other family members you have seen—unreasonable, demanding, hysterical—and in your effort not to play that role (especially before your colleagues), you find yourself behaving like a doctor—or like some strange parody of a doctor—rather than a parent.

One interesting twist on the idea of doctorly authority and parental limitations was offered by an article that appeared in the April 1991 issue of *Pediatrics*. The authors described a 5-year-old girl who had been spanked by her mother with a wooden paddle and had bled subcutaneously to such an extent that she presented in hypovolemic shock. The authors took the opportunity to inveigh against corporal punishment, reminding their readers of all the possible physical injuries and bad psychological effects that can result from spanking.

The physicians who wrote in to protest this article were not, needless to say, defending what had happened to the little girl. One doctor wrote, "Pediatricians, as scientists, cannot dismiss a centuries-old practice which has deep roots in Judaeo-Christian culture strictly on the basis of anecdotal reports of injury when physical punishment obviously is carried much too far." It would be, he argued, like looking at antibiotics only through the window of the most serious side effects possible. He went on to recommend certain criteria for the use of physical punishment—the same criteria he recommends to parents in his practice.

The next letter was frankly angry. The author, another pediatrician, demanded to know whom the authors of the original article thought they had helped by publishing the case. He wrote: "I feel quite certain that one person the authors have not helped is the health care professional who is the author of this letter. I have been married for nearly 18 years and have raised three children to the ages of 14, 11, and 10 years. Although I have not used corporal punishment with great frequency, I readily admit I have spanked my children when I felt they willfully disobeyed. I do not recall I have ever used more than five strokes, and I have never produced more than transient erythema of the backside and a brief profusion of tears."

In reading this exchange of letters, what I recognized was this: we feel, as physicians, a need to be experts, and to defend what we do. This is important with patients. But it is nearly impossible to be experts with our own children because parents' behavior is shaped by upbringing, cultural context, by all the intense echoes of our personal experience and profound conviction. The application of medical literature to normal life is fraught with tension.

Recently I read a letter in *The New England Journal of Medicine* from a physician who had learned that at some hospitals, children are allowed to accompany their mothers and witness the birth of younger siblings. The physician was very upset by what he felt was obviously a traumatic and dangerous experience for these children, and he urged his colleagues to help put a stop to it. Reading this letter, I felt personally attacked because my 5-year-old—at his own request, after all—came to the hospital when I went into labor with his little sister.

I began to mentally compose a letter of response. I would tell, I thought, the story of how I took my son to a birthing class to watch the movie so he could see for himself how bloody and painful childbirth is. All around us were very pregnant women and their extremely supportive partners, and when the movie was over, almost everyone was in tears—this is the first time most people see childbirth, and many see it when they are very close to having the experience themselves. I looked down at my son. Was he moved? Was he grossed out? He looked up at me. "Are we going to McDonald's before we go home?" he asked.

I was sure the readers of the *New England Journal* would find this amusing. But the point is, I felt defensive. Here was something in the medical literature more or less assailing my own expertise as a mother and as a pediatrician. I had to defend myself, had to show that I did what I did from a platform of knowledge and understanding, not, like other parents, improvising and guessing and doing the best I could.

In Mary McCarthy's *The Group*, Priss and Sloan Crockett raise a well-regulated child but for one serious lapse. Little Stephen eats a proper child diet and follows a proper child schedule. But there is one thing he will not do, and it is the thing that his mother is forbidden to punish by all the canons of modern child-rearing: "As the wife of a pediatrician, she was bitterly ashamed that Stephen, at the age of two and a half, was not able to control his bowels. He not only made evil-smelling messes in his bed, at nap time, but he sometimes soiled his pants here in the Park. . . . Or he did it—like last weekend—in his bathing trunks on the beach at the Oyster Bay clubhouse, in front of the whole summer colony, who were sunning and having cocktails. Sloan, even though he was a doctor, was extremely annoyed whenever Stephen did it in public, but he would never help Priss clean Stephen up or do anything to relieve her embarrassment."

It is Priss's horrified fantasy that her son is rebelling by refusing to be toilet-trained, taking revenge on her for all the things he has been denied in the name of proper child-rearing practices, the schedule he was held to so rigorously, the pacifier he was denied. "For the fact, in short, that his father was a pediatrician."

Raising children is joyful and educational, but also frightening and frustrating. As physicians, we learn ways to deal with fear, uncertainty, and medical ambiguity. But in raising our own children, worrying over the dilemmas of healthy family life and agonizing through their illnesses, we are exposed to a more complex—and ultimately educational—tangle of fear, love, and ambiguity.

My daughter had terrible difficulties with separation at bedtime; she would always ask for one more story, one more story. She had all these inventive ways of prolonging bedtime, like asking for some toy she knew was lost. Eventually it got to the point where there were long bouts of crying every night, and my wife and I were increasingly angry and helpless. I felt stupid. This is something I deal with all the time with other parents: I tell them firmly and with great conviction, "Put the child in bed, let the child cry for 10 minutes . . . "

What ended up happening with us was that Grandma came to visit. She sat in the room and sang to my daughter and talked to her until she fell asleep, and bedtimes got defused. Then we went on from there, and we dealt with the problem of always needing to have someone in the room. And I learned that there's no substitute for a good grandma.

—Pediatrician, age 32

CHAPTER FIVE

YOUR PARENTS,
YOUR DOCTORS

Every doctor has to be on call every once in a while and she usually gets home late. Having a doctor for a mother is kind of fun, but there's also disadvantages. I was about 5 or 6 when I began to understand about being on call. I understood that she had to work late. I always used to think there was like an emergency. You can save lives and stop great suffering and it makes you feel good, and she's usually happy when she did something good.

If I can't become a pro sportswriter or a musician then I'll probably be a doctor. It runs in the family and I want to keep the tradition going. A friend of ours, a doctor, was complaining that basketball players get paid millions of dollars to shoot a ball through a hoop and he saves lives and doesn't get half that much. But saving lives is a wonderful thing to do.

I have a personal feeling about the hospital smell—it's unique. I think it's kind of a neat smell.

You have a better relationship with your doctors, especially if you go to a hospital where your mom or dad works. Everyone knows you. I think they're very good with children in the Boston area. I think they have the best hospitals in the U.S.

—Daniel, age 11

n 1962, Dr. Benjamin Spock contributed to *Pediatrics* an essay with the then-provocative title, "Should Not Physicians' Families Be Allowed the Comfort of Paying for Medical Care?" He argued that the common practice of professional courtesy—doctors caring for other doctors and their families without charge—was dangerous because it led to insufficient medical care. Spock's hypothetical doctor worried about whether an illness was worth bringing to the attention of a peer: "He cannot, unless he is a most unusual person, detach himself emotionally while he takes a history and does a physical examination. His natural anxiety tends to make him vacillate between exaggerating and minimizing the significance of the symptom. From the start he is debating in his mind whether it would be appropriate to call the proper physician. Consciously or unconsciously he is wondering how that colleague would view the request for help. Is the condition one with which he himself would be considered competent or incompetent to deal? If it proves insignificant will he be thought an alarmist, a neurotic? Or if he tries to deal with it himself and it turns out to be serious, will he seem a bungler? His male pride makes him not wish to ask for unnecessary assistance, and his human dislike of imposing urges him to at least procrastinate. While his mind is distracted by these issues he edges toward a hazy kind of diagnosis, on the basis of a partial examination or none at all."

Spock argued that the doctor's wife, even without the benefit of medical training, was more likely to see clearly when medical help was needed: "If she is like most women, she is too sensible to have such a vulnerable pride about asking for help." However, her husband's medical authority would likely overrule her sensible instincts; his hesitation and self-consciousness would prevent her from doing what she felt was necessary. And while this was problem enough when it came to physical illness, Spock continued, it was even more serious with psychiatric and developmental problems (which are by definition chinks in the physician's armor).

Spock thought that many of these conflicts and confusions were attributable to the fact that one doctor, in calling another, was asking a favor. Rather than a professional service with reimbursement, it was a transaction that involved a "close to obligatory" Christmas present in return for services rendered. It is now far more common for doctors to pay for health care, but many of the confusions persist. And though it is now more likely than it once was that the doctor will be female, her medical training may have replaced the native good sense in which Spock placed his trust.

Frankly, I recognize his description of the doctor agonizing over a family member—it describes some of the convolutions I go through myself in deciding whether or not to call the pediatrician. Will he think I should have been able to handle it? Will he think I should have called him a long time ago? Will he pick up something

I have missed? Even when we meet over the sick body of my child, the pediatrician is my professional colleague, and I cannot help imagining his assessment.

During residency, we used to groan when we had to admit a doctor's kid. True, we used to groan even more dramatically about admitting a lawyer's kid (or worse, the child of two lawyers), but we didn't really like dealing with doctors as parents. Some of them stick in my mind—the internist whose child had a mysterious neurologic problem, for example. This doctor, on his own initiative, had consulted adult neurologists, rheumatologists, and infectious-disease specialists from the hospital where he had trained and therefore knew "the best people." So the best people self-consciously came over to our hospital to examine the poor child and apologetically explain that as nonpediatricians they didn't know much about children. They would inevitably make a couple of suggestions and then bow out; the child's father would think of another potentially relevant subspecialty and make a few calls.

Or take the geneticist whose infant daughter developed a high fever and was admitted for a sepsis workup. As it turned out, the geneticist's wife was what we called a crunchy-granola person—she didn't believe in artificial substances like antibiotics and was worried that the various procedures involved in the workup would traumatize her daughter to a point where full psychological recovery would be impossible. The mother put the intern through an extensive catechism: Why is it necessary to draw blood? Why can't you just take the urine out of the bag instead of traumatizing her with a catheter? Does there really have to be an IV? And the whole time the geneticist father sat quietly, looking uncomfortable; the baby's well-being was obviously primarily his wife's department. Oh, how we wanted him to step in and reassure her that we weren't monsters, that we weren't making all this up just to traumatize her baby. When he didn't, we were furious at him.

My sister says she never realized the cost and bureaucracy of the medical system. She put her arm through a glass door once, and our father drove her to the hospital. He knew everyone, and he walked right in and said, "I've got a patient for you." And once she needed her leg X-rayed, and she didn't have to wait. She never realized what it's really like for patients, not till she was working and had insurance of her own.

—Research assistant, age 30

There is no question that doctors' children exist in a medically privileged environment. Though it may be a somewhat dubious privilege to have double sets of subspecialists coming out of the woodwork, it is still a mark of special attention. There is, however, a very fine line between the privilege of having a parent who can arrange special treatment and the burden of having a parent who *insists* on arranging special treatment.

In a 1988 essay published in the *Canadian Medical Association Journal*, Dr. James McSherry offered a perspective from the field of university health services, a field in which, he said, he took care of many other doctors' children. "During my years in the student health field I have come to recognize the phrase 'My father (or mother, or, even worse, both!) is a doctor' as the harbinger of some out-of-the-ordinary clinical experience." He went on to identify what he called the "MD-parent syndrome," explaining that this syndrome "only comes to full flower when the MD-parent's child consults a physician the parent does not know, and is therefore seen only in a *forme fruste* by the doctors the MD-parent has chosen as suitable attending physicians."

In other words, McSherry argued, some physician parents are never able to bring themselves to trust other doctors or to allow their children the independence of making health-care decisions for themselves. He divided parents suffering from the syndrome into three levels of severity. At the first level are parents who act as their children's primary physicians, producing erratic or incomplete medical records and immunization histories that are either "incomplete or overenthusiastic." At the second level are parents who take active control of their children's health care even when the children are away from home, seeking copies of all medical records and exercising the right of veto over all medical decisions. At the third and most severe level are parents who exhibit all the behaviors of the first two levels and also use financial control or family loyalty to reinforce their absolute authority over all aspects of their children's care.

Quite reasonably, McSherry concluded that "The problem does not lie with the physician who is a parent, but with certain parents who are physicians—they would have the same fundamental need for dependency and control were they factory workers, or lawyers." It may be especially hard for doctors to acknowledge their children's increasing independence when it comes to health-related issues. A doctor who takes pride in the fact that his patients freely confide even sensitive details of their lives, relying on his medical confidentiality and open-mindedness, may be genuinely taken aback when a teenage son refuses to avail himself of the same privilege.

> *Once my dad's nurse had a cardiac arrest and dropped dead in his office. He asked me to take her place temporarily and started having me buzz people in and answer phones. I would be there for gynecologic exams. I was really shocked. I was 14 or 15, and I had never had a gynecologic exam, and then he was handing me the white coat.*
>
> *It was my mother who explained the facts of life, though my father was present. He wasn't very explicit, but he was sometimes incredibly direct about bodily functions—it could be embarrassing. I mean, he was direct in a medical way.*
>
> —Research assistant, age 30

Of course, doctors as parents are often perfectly normal—anxious and loving, confused and protective. Sometimes they are obnoxious, demanding, and entitled—the way the orthopedic resident probably thought I was when I demanded a special pain regimen for my own son. In fact, what he said to me during that middle-of-the-night consultation was this: "Ten thousand kids have fractures; they all get IM morphine for pain. Why is this kid different?" And my reply (I was trying for medical dignity, but achieving only a semi-fanatical calm) was this: "Because this kid is *my* kid, and I know there is a better way."

> *We all went to the pediatrician for routine stuff, but Dad would prescribe medication for allergies. My mom was impressed that I was involved in and present at the deliveries of both my kids—she went on and on about it—because my dad wasn't. He said that was a transaction between my mother and her OB.*
>
> —Internist, age 33

In a 1991 study published in *The New England Journal of Medicine*, Dr. John La Puma and colleagues surveyed the members of the medical staff of a community teaching hospital to see how many had been asked for medical advice or treatment by family members, how many had given it, and whether they had special concerns about such treatment. Ninety-nine percent of the 465 physicians in the study reported having been asked for medical help by a family member, 59 percent by their children. Forty-four doctors had operated

"As long as I have a water tap, a flame, and some blotting paper, I can just as well work in a barn."

Miles is proud to present this series on...

Powerful Innovators

Powerful Physician

Paul Ehrlich (1854-1915)

Even as a child, Ehrlich displayed the curiosity and imagination we associate with brilliant scientists. His vivid descriptions earned him the nickname "Dr. Fantasy."

Ehrlich proved a gifted, intuitive experimenter who astonished his colleagues with the accuracy of his work.

In 1908, Ehrlich was awarded a share of the Nobel Prize in medicine and physiology for his research on immunity and serum. He spent the better part of two decades studying chemicals to find those that would selectively kill bacteria without harming humans. Interestingly, his most famous discovery came after he won the Nobel Prize, when he identified a compound known as "606"—naming it Salvasan (from salvation)—and identified its usefulness against syphilis—one of the most feared, albeit least discussed, diseases at that time.

Ehrlich's work marked the beginning of modern chemotherapy. Many believe that he set in motion the quick discovery of cures for many infectious diseases.

Powerful Antimicrobial

Today, in lower respiratory infections,* some pathogens are no longer routinely susceptible to traditional agents. One important reason the power of Cipro® stands out is its unique mode of action. It allows the power of Cipro® to remain unaffected by ß-lactamase or plasmid-mediated resistance. And cross-resistance, which often limits the usefulness of other classes of antibiotics, is not a problem reported with Cipro®. In fact, Cipro® kills susceptible pathogens* during all four phases of cell growth.[†]

Cipro® TABLETS
(ciprofloxacin HCl)

The most potent fluoroquinolone.[1-3‡]

*Due to susceptible strains of indicated pathogens. See indicated organisms in prescribing information.
[†]Data on file, Miles Inc Pharmaceutical Division.
[‡]*In vitro* activity does not necessarily imply a correlation with *in vivo* results.

See full prescribing information at the end of this book.

Powerful Numbers

Speak for themselves

12 *...The number of hours serum concentrations of Cipro® are maintained in excess of $MIC_{90}s$ of most susceptible bacteria.*

96 *...The percentage of favorable clinical response (resolution + improvement) with Cipro® in lower respiratory infections due to susceptible strains of indicated pathogens.*

250/500/750 *...Dosage strengths of Cipro® Tablets available.*

Cipro® TABLETS

(ciprofloxacin HCI)

The most potent fluoroquinolone.[1-3‡]

CIPRO® SHOULD NOT BE USED IN CHILDREN, ADOLESCENTS, OR PREGNANT WOMEN.

See full prescribing information at the end of this book.

MILES Ⱥ

Pharmaceutical Division

Miles Inc.
Pharmaceutical Division
400 Morgan Lane
West Haven, CT 06516

on a family member, seven of those on their children. (Though the article does not specify which operations were performed on children, many of the procedures cited were dermatologic, and few would require general anesthesia.) Thirty-eight of the respondents had treated family members with major medical illnesses, and eight of these cases involved their own children.

In discussing the sources of discomfort that physicians reported in providing medical care to family members, the authors of the study brought up doctors' need to set limits and the difficulty of maintaining those limits when close relatives are involved. "Our data suggest that along with limiting their active participation, physicians attempt to limit their emotional involvement in family members' care. Setting limits may reflect physicians' recognition of the emotional complexity of having dual roles, physicans' difficulty in providing reassurance when a serious illness is suspected, or the problems anticipated when there is a family relationship instead of a potentially therapeutic doctor-patient relationship."

The doctors in the study were not all taking care of their children, of course. Many were caring for parents, in-laws, or siblings. However, it could be argued that those who were doctoring their children were involved in the most complex relationship of all. The normal relationship between adult siblings, for example, does not include a great deal of medical caretaking. In contrast, the normal parent-child relationship involves frequent, small semimedical attentions—taking temperatures, attending to rashes, administering medicine, monitoring diet and bowel habits, and generally promoting the growth of a healthy body and a strong spirit. Therefore, the line is less clearly drawn when it comes to physicians using their medical skills on their own children. Feeling the forehead is any parent's prerogative. But how about taking the pulse? Doctoring your own child may not add a new element to the standard equation, but it makes a simple constant into a complex variable.

Further, it is hard to limit your emotional involvement when it comes to your own child; it is probably harder to be objective than it is with any other family member. There is the extra weight of responsibility, the strong sense that—regardless of medical training—you are *already* supposed to be in charge of caring and protecting and making everything all better.

My dad is very intelligent and erudite, very quietly compassion-
ate. He's very interested in medical ethics, end-of-life decisions.
When his father died from a stroke, we were on vacation. He lin-

*gered on for three weeks, with Dad commuting back and forth, try-
ing to deal with his dad dying and also with medical decisions.*

*He was on the medical staff where I went to medical school and
did my residency. He would illustrate things with stories about me
and my brother. I heard more than I ever had before. My brother
was born transiently hemiparetic after a difficult delivery, and my
dad likes to use this as an example for discussing ethical issues—
in particular to show that my brother had a rough start and he's
done fine, to illustrate that you can't always make the decision.*

—Internist, age 33

All the complexities of being both a physician and a parent—
the confusion of roles, the normal defenses, the defenses instilled
by medical training, the disjunction between professional vocabulary and natural emotion—are intensified when a physician's child
becomes seriously ill, or even dies. At that time, a parent must reach
for any emotional props at all and use whatever personal and professional supports exist to handle anxiety and grief.

Dr. Rebecca R. Tomsyck, writing in a 1988 issue of *The Journal of
the American Medical Women's Association*, examined her experience
with the birth and death of her own premature infant during her
second year in pediatric practice. She had had no problems during
the pregnancy, and with her husband had been looking forward to
the baby. "There was security in the fact that I was a pediatrician; I
would make a good mother." Then at 22 weeks she developed some
fluid leakage, and at 26 weeks the fluid became purulent and labor
had to be induced. In her medical voice she wrote, "A premature
male infant with no gross physical abnormalities was delivered and
lived approximately two hours."

Many physicians retreat into this medical voice when describing
their own medical problems or those of their children. It is the vocabulary we know best, the vocabulary that answers the questions
we are trained to ask. It can, I suppose, restore a semblance of control and of medical detachment. When my son broke his leg, I answered inquiries from doctors by saying, "He has a spiral fracture
of his femur." I answered inquiries from everyone else by saying,
"He broke his leg." When doctors come to a pediatrician for help,
they tend to talk in the formal cadences of a physician presenting
a patient.

It was Tomsyck's intention to contrast this detached voice with
her account of what she was really feeling. In her nonmedical, personal voice, she described the misery and guilt she endured when

she learned that her membranes had ruptured. "Why me? What had I done to deserve such punishment? I had spent almost five years as a pediatrician taking care of other mothers' children, why was this happening to mine? When I was a pediatric intern, exhausted, working alone at night in the intensive care nursery, I would find myself thinking, *If this baby would just die tonight instead of in the morning I could rest for a few minutes.* I reasoned this was my unpardonable sin; now my baby was dying and I was responsible." She went on to castigate herself for the long hours she had worked during pregnancy, the infectious diseases she had allowed herself to be exposed to, the postponement of pregnancy to complete her medical training.

She described her decision that the infant should not be resuscitated, how she felt torn between what she believed was right as a physician and what she desperately wanted as a mother. Finally, movingly, she described what happened in the delivery room: "When they gave me my tiny, but perfectly formed baby it was as though someone had doused me with ice water. Suddenly, as my defenses failed, I was confronted with the reality that my baby was born, but would soon die. I had failed as a woman, a mother, a physician. When my husband came in we wept together in the otherwise silent delivery room. . . . Part of me yearned to hold the tiny baby close to comfort him as he struggled to live. Another part of me wanted to palpate his abdomen, feel his fontanel, check his Moro. I inquired into the possibility of Trisomy 21, or the need for an autopsy; I asked that chromosomal studies be done. As a mother I yearned to hold my child and to have him live, as a physician I knew his death was inevitable." At the moment of tragedy the stark conflict between her two identities was most devastatingly irreconcilable.

The death of her child wounded her as a mother. She had failed to do the thing that every mother wants to do: deliver a healthy baby. But also, Tomsyck wrote, she had been wounded in her identity as a physician, someone who could help, someone who had always been the recipient of thanks from grateful families. Her omnipotence was destroyed; she could not save the child she most wanted to save. She could only decide that there would be no aggressive intervention. And while her training and experience as a pediatrician helped make it a much more educated decision than it might have been for another parent, they did not make it any less agonizing.

I might suggest that another element in her sorrow was that her profession had let her down. Perhaps she felt that not only had she failed, but all of medicine had failed. She needed what so many patients need in extremis—she needed something medicine cannot do. You might say "cannot do *yet*," but that doesn't really matter to the parent who needs a treatment for a childhood malignancy right now, a therapy for cystic fibrosis right now, or a way to keep a 24-weeker safe and uninfected and inside the womb right now.

Like virtually every physician who has written about the experience of illness, Tomsyck concluded by reflecting that her grief left her a more understanding physician. She lost most of her sense of omnipotence, she wrote, but gained a new appreciation of the preciousness and the precariousness of life. This is, in the end, exactly what our children do for us: they expose us, the hard way, to all the terrors of illness and accident. They expose us to all the variables we cannot control, we who have chosen a profession that sets such a premium on control. And they expose us not through danger to ourselves—that can usually be handled by bravado and denial—but through danger to those we love, those we would give anything to protect and defend. Some doctors try to defend their children professionally by caring for their health, and it is probably true that this can be a gesture of control as well as an offering of love and convenience. As parents, doctors labor under special burdens, expected by others and expecting themselves to wield their medical omnipotence on behalf of those they love.

Perhaps it would be appropriate to close with the famous opening line of Dr. Spock's *Baby and Child Care*, a book that helped educate and reassure many parents operating without benefit of medical training: "You know more than you think you do." For physician parents the opposite may be true—we may sometimes know less than we think we do.

CHAPTER SIX

TIME AND TIMING

My father was gone a lot—I can't remember a weekend he didn't go in. And he was always going away to meetings. It was a big stress for my mom because she had to handle four of us, and it was a thing they would argue about. My mother has mixed feelings about her kids becoming doctors, because of her own experiences. You can tell at times that she's thinking there's a negative aspect of it, that it takes a lot of time.

I had my kids when I was a first-year fellow and then at the end of the fellowship. With my wife now, time is a big stress between the two of us, especially because I have to moonlight a lot—I'm gone seven nights a month. It's tough on my older daughter. She understands what a doctor is, and that I'm not one of those nasty ones that sticks things in her ears. I've taken her with me to do consults at a local hospital. And part of my reason for choosing this academic track is that the hours are probably better in the long run.

I'd like my kids to get a sense that what I do is important to me—I like taking care of people and making them better.

—Internist, age 33

hen I spoke to doctors and to adult children of doctors, the theme that came up most often and most predictably was time: Never enough time. Always away. Always pressed for time. Children of male doctors and children of female doctors, doctor mothers and doctor fathers, everyone had the same complaint. The question of time seems to be part of every child's memories, however affectionate, and part of every parent's worries.

In 1987, surgeon Margaret Levy wrote in *JAMA*'s "A Piece of My Mind" column: "Now comes the woman who thinks she can have a rewarding career in medicine and—at the same time—raise a family. Let me tell you, once and for all, that this is neither physically nor psychologically possible." Her choice, she wrote, had been to be a full-time surgeon, while her husband was a full-time parent to their two sons. They had made this choice because day-care kids "are absolutely pathetic, no matter how good the day care is."

Naturally, other doctors wrote in to angrily defend their own lives, their day-care kids, the choices they had made. These can be confusing times, with people choosing among a complex array of options for how to live a life, for how to combine two lives into a couple, and for how to raise children. One sad consequence is that many become furiously defensive of the balance they ultimately strike. Whatever you are doing must be the single best thing to do; all other options must plainly be flawed. They must result in doom, devastation, and despair—or at least pathetic children, broken marriages, and ruined careers.

The problem of time is not new, and not strictly an issue raised because more doctors are now women. It's the logical outcome of a profession that is also a vocation, that is subject to the overwhelming exigencies of life and death, and that sets a high standard on dedication, availability, and compulsive hard work. When I spoke to adult children of doctors—people who had grown up with fathers who were full-time doctors and mothers who were full-time mothers—they all maintained that their fathers had been away too much. To choose medicine, to make it into and through medical school, and to manage residency, you have to be hard-working, willing to delay gratification, and more than a little obsessed with your work. In fact, "compulsive" is a compliment in residency: "She's very compulsive" is high praise for an intern, while "He's not particularly compulsive" means he is not on top of his patients.

You are rewarded for your hard work with more hard work, of course, but also with the responsibility you wanted. And with that responsibility you can find reason to work even harder. Though your family may resent how hard you work, they have to acknowledge how important that work is. There is a particular emotional hurdle in this, in the guilt that people feel if they resent a doctor's absence. True, there are promises being broken at home, but perhaps there are lives being saved somewhere else!

In *Hippocrates' Handmaidens*, Nitzberg spends a great deal of time on the issue of physicians who are always gone, who are unavailable to their wives and children. A doctor's wife, she says, must always be willing to wait patiently, and always be ready to see her plans disrupted. "What appears to underlie this waiting and accommo-dating is the clear message that the doctor's time is most impor-tant and valuable. Have you noticed how all people will graciously accept a doctor's tardiness? No one expresses anger or disap-pointment when he enters a room, party, or meeting late. Rather, he is greeted with reverence and great curiosity as to his latest con-quest in the world of medicine."

> *My father was in solo practice, in general internal medicine. He had people covering when he needed to leave town, but otherwise he was always on call for his own practice. He would leave really early and wouldn't come home until after six. He put a lot of time into it, now that I think back. On holidays, his beeper would go off and he would have to go to the hospital. He'd end up getting up in the middle of the night three or four times a week. He never complained—and maybe we didn't sympathize enough. And when I become a doctor, if I have to go through that, well, I wouldn't complain because it was what I wanted to do. But I realize my fa-ther spent a lot of time at work. I didn't see him except for vaca-tions. He went to the hospital every single day—he still does.*
> —Research assistant, age 30

When doctors, male and female, are asked to identify sources of conflict in their marriages, their demanding schedules are cited most often. It has, however, been suggested in the literature that these long hours are effect, not cause—that is, that physicians work the schedules they work at least in part to escape from their fami-lies, from domestic conflicts and tensions.

In 1987, Dr. Glen O. Gabbard and colleagues studied physician marriages (as in most studies, the majority of the couples consisted of a male physician and a female nonphysician) and concluded, as have other researchers, that there is no apparent correlation be-tween longer working hours and increased marital conflict. The physicians in their study did tend to consider the amount of time they spent away from home an important source of strain—in fact, they rated it much higher as a stress than did their spouses. The spouses were more concerned about a lack of intimacy and com-munication on the part of their (mostly) husbands.

In 1991, Dr. Cynda A. Johnson and others studied 21 British cou-ples in which both partners were physicians. These doctors iden-tified the greatest source of conflict in their marriages as the amount of time the husband spent at work. The wife's hours were felt to be a much less severe stress—possibly because many of the wives in the study worked more limited hours. The authors hypothesized that the husbands' hours caused such severe stress because "the women wanted more domestic help from their husbands, both partners wanted the husbands to spend more time with their wives and children, or the women who had made willing career compromises for children or marriage still felt some degree of resentment over that decision."

Whether time constraints are a cause or an effect of marital stress, they seem to be a common and blatant source of parental strain. When doctors, male or female, discuss their children, the conversation almost always turns to time—to the school plays missed and promises broken, to the late-to-pick-up-at-the-babysitter dilemma and the anxiety over who will stay home if a child gets sick.

> *Last night my son and I were lying there together and he said, "You're never here." He's right—and I'm there more than most doctors. I'm a single parent, a widow, and I feel a lot of pressure. I work part time; I'm supposed to have one day a week off, but I'm always at work. I didn't go into private practice because I couldn't keep the time commitment.*
>
> *Nobody can do everything; even if you try, something invariably doesn't get done. I felt very strongly that I wanted to be with my children. Did that affect my academic career? Absolutely. Does it put pressure on me? Absolutely. But my philosophy is that the only person who really cares about your kids is you. Time is the biggest burden, not money.*
>
> *My son watches me—he doesn't understand why I can't be there, unless it has to do with a sick patient. The lab and research are not being a doctor. Being a doctor is when you see a patient.*
>
> —Pediatrician, age 42

When I was a resident, I didn't take sick days for my own ailments. It was a relatively civilized residency program, as these things go, with a sick-call system. Since I covered for others, I knew I was entitled to a day off now and then if I needed it. The thing was, I also knew I would eventually need those days for my son's illnesses. Most of the extra work devolved onto Larry, but it was understood that I would cover if he had a lecture to give. So I hoarded my sick days, working when I had the flu (yes, I know, breathing flu virus into the faces of small, sick children).

Those of us who had small children during residency spent our days trying to get done, to get out of the hospital, to get home. Of course, the other residents were mostly doing that too, but I think those of us who were parents felt a stronger, more anxious drive. At the same time, we were more likely to feel guilty about our eagerness to leave, more likely to feel that it would be interpreted as a lack of dedication. There was a man in my program who kept an eye on the clock all day long, eager to get to the gym and work out, and I don't think he ever felt anyone would doubt his commitment to medicine just because he loved his Nautilus machines. On the other hand, it seemed possible that anyone whose main priority was getting home in time to see a child before bedtime would be viewed as having divided loyalties.

I have various bad memories from residency, days when I made mistakes, or when bad things happened to my patients. Here is one of the days I absolutely cannot bear to remember, a day I simply blocked out of my memory for several years: My schedule had been changed around, and I found myself working in the ER during a month that had originally been allotted to elective. Because it was supposed to be my elective month, Larry had planned a brief trip out of town to a conference, figuring I would be able to cope with our son alone for a couple of days. But instead I was in the ER. So I got Benjamin to the day-care center before the doors opened and drove to the hospital, arriving 45 minutes late for morning conference. During the morning, more scheduling confusions prompted an angry lecture from one of the ER attendings—a woman I liked very much—who accused me of not taking my ER duties seriously. At the end of the day, I rushed everyone through sign-out rounds, risked offending the same attending again, and drove like a crazy person to get to the day-care center only 15 minutes late for pickup. I brought my son home and collapsed in tears of self-pity; all day long I had said nothing but "I'm sorry, I'm sorry, I can't help it, I'm sorry." And now here I was at home with my child, and all I wanted to do was sit on the couch and sniffle.

Once again, I am citing residency because it was like real life only more so. Now that I am no longer a resident, I find that life only rarely reaches that pitch of I-can't-do-this, that histrionic self-reproach mixed with self-pity. Still, tinges are always there, because there is still never enough time.

Anything beyond a reasonable number of hours—and you know that's already too many hours most of the time—and I would feel it begin to stretch my limits, feel it taking something away from my wife and my kids, and it would make me angry. I was never short-tempered with my patients, but I would feel very frustrated and angry inside. The result was that I became incredibly efficient, with my goal always to do my best for the patients at work and then go home and do my best for my kids. This may all have something to do with my being the child of a physician, a child who sometimes felt ignored by my father. He used the easy excuse of, "I have to go to the hospital," and then I wouldn't see him again.

—Internist, age 33

Children can be a full-time job. At the very least, they demand a whole-life adaptation. It has been suggested that one factor contributing to stress for female physicians is that their natures—competitive, driven, perfectionistic—cause them to aim for some extreme state of achievement both as parents and professionals.

On the other hand, many women are thought to make alterations in their medical careers in order to accommodate their family lives. There is the standing dilemma of when to have children in the first place. As Dr. M. Andrew Greganti and Dr. Suzanne W. Fletcher wrote to the *Annals of Internal Medicine* in 1985, "Medical residency comes during a time that is physiologically best for beginning a family and beyond which there is an increasing risk of a poor pregnancy outcome. If a woman physician is to have children during her 20's, pregnancy and child care are bound to coincide with some aspect of her medical training, be it medical school, residency, or fellowship, or the beginning of practice or an academic career." It is a truism among women in academic medicine that the period after training is a dicey time to have children since it is supposed to be a period of frenzied research and publishing, the years in which you build a career. Similarly, many physicians have mixed feelings about becoming pregnant during their first years in a practice when they are trying to cultivate the trust and good opinion of those with whom they work.

Dr. Maureen Sayres, writing in *The New England Journal of Medicine* in 1986, summed up the issues that militate against childbearing for the female physician (she was speaking particularly about residency, but once again, by extension, her words apply to other stages of a medical career): "The current climate of residency is in direct conflict with the realities of a young person's life—the time needed to develop a relationship with a partner; the age limits of fertility; the time needed to carry, breast-feed, and care for a baby; and the need to sleep in order to function effectively." I think all doctor parents have had the experience of coming home from work, eager to be with the family and play with the kids, and immediately falling asleep.

Then there is the choice of medical field; family and career issues are thought to influence the demographics of medicine. Women opt in large numbers to enter primary-care fields, and comparatively few go into surgery. This is often explained as an unwillingness on the part of women to enter training programs and disciplines that, by their severity, render family life almost impossible. Dr. Steven C. Martin and colleagues, writing in *The Western Journal of Medicine* in 1988, commented that "The structure of medical training and professional advancement inhibits or even penalizes persons who seek to devote substantial time to personal commitments. . . . Our society continues to place a disproportionate emphasis on women's domestic responsibilities. The logical response of many women physicians is to seek careers that are more amenable to integrating their personal and professional lives." Implicit in this observation is the axiom that doctors themselves will have to make the adjustments that allow for integration, that the profession itself is not going to compromise its demands.

It seems clear that family considerations influence specialty choice and career path for many male physicians as well; it is not at all uncommon to meet men who have made choices that enable them to support their families in style and to have more time away from work. But when men make these decisions the issues are less likely to be called family and career dilemmas and more likely to be termed lifestyle considerations. Somehow, the phrase *lifestyle considerations* conjures up the doctor's desire to have enough time to devote to his richly fulfilling cultural interests and athletic pursuits—opera and golf, perhaps—while making enough money to live in a style of civilized comfort.

In some studies of how children and family affect career choice, men have been entirely ignored; that is to say, they have been used as an implicit control group, the guardians of the null hypothesis. It is assumed that these considerations have no effect on men; therefore, if they affect women, the women must be different. Other studies, however, have looked at both male and female doctors.

In one Canadian study, published in a 1988 issue of the *Journal of the American Medical Women's Association*, Dr. May Cohen and colleagues surveyed graduates of McMaster University Medical School to examine the factors that influenced their career development.

This group of physicians entered practice in the late 1970s and the 1980s. There was a great deal of overlap between the men and women in terms of which factors helped their careers and which hindered, but none of the men identified interference by family and children as a disadvantage. The authors commented: "It had been anticipated that as more women pursued careers, family and child care responsibilities would increasingly become a shared responsibility. Our sample failed to demonstrate this; the problem is still perceived as such only by women and, presumably, is also viewed as a problem for women."

My whole notion of having a child changed when I had my daughter—also my ideas about wanting to work full time. It's a selfish thing; it's because of the tremendous pleasure she gives me. There's nothing in my work environment which gives me the same kind of pleasure.

—Obstetrician, age 31

In addition to their underrepresentation within medicine, more women than men choose to work as employees rather than open their own practices, and they are more likely to work part time. These choices are often seen as responses to the exigencies of family life. In 1987, Dr. Carol S. Weisman and Dr. Martha A. Teitelbaum surveyed 1,420 ob-gyns, half of them male and half female, and found that the married men in the study reported working a mean of 69.3 hours per week, while the married women reported a mean of 61.8 hours. The number of children had a negative but statistically nonsignificant effect on the number of hours worked each week by the women, while the male doctors worked approximately 1.7 hours more per week per additional child. It is impossible to tell from the data whether these trends reflect increased economic pressure on fathers of larger families (leading to an extra 1.7 hours of work a week?), fathers' attempts to escape their family responsibilities and stresses, or no particularly profound meaning at all. It would, of course, be somewhat ironic if a group of women working more than 60 hours a week while also maintaining families should somehow be seen as slacking off.

When my mother is on call, me and my father go to a restaurant after school, or we go bowling. Often we'll have a simple dinner of noodles.

—Benjamin, age 7

The imperatives of a medical career influence the amount and type of time that a parent spends with a child. Children of doctors, by and large, grow up knowing that the sound of a beeper may call a parent away. Medical parents, especially mothers, but also fathers, can find themselves desperately conscious of the constraints of time, the constant stress of managing a job that cannot be easily contained while saving time for their own children. Conversely, the imperatives of childbearing and child-rearing influence medical career decisions for many of us—again, especially for women, but also for men. Life from day to day, from year to year, from one professional stage to another, becomes a question of timing.

CONCLUSION

Dad is chief of neurology at the university. I can't remember not being aware of Dad as a doctor. When I was little he would take me in on weekends, not to see patients, but to play in the office. And when I was 7 or 8, I had a standing offer to have an EMG performed on myself, which I always turned down—I had seen the long needles. In high school sometime I decided to be a doctor. I was always interested in science, and I had exposure to my dad as a role model.

Watching him when I was in medical school reinforced my idea of how he would interact with patients. In class they would bring in patients and Dad was always very solicitous and respectful. Some of the other people treated the patients more like exhibits.

As an intern, my first rotation was on his neurology service— my residency director's idea of a joke. He is a very nonthreatening teacher. He'll ask a question, you'll struggle, and after 10 seconds he'll say, "Well, what you're undoubtedly thinking of is . . . "

And he's probably one of the best physical diagnosticians I've known. My first night alone I had 11 admissions—I was in the CT scanner with the 10th, and the 11th was in the helicopter with Guillain-Barré syndrome and respiratory failure; I called my father to complain. He told me, "Stop whining; you're here to learn and you should be enjoying this!"

—Internist, age 33

octors come into frequent, intimate contact with diseases, accidents, disabilities, and bad outcomes. To survive exposure to these constant reminders of human vulnerability, most of us practice denial: *This will not happen to me.* Children are a great big crack in that defense; it is hard to deny that children are human and vulnerable. They are assignments in caretaking for doctors who may have done very little laying on of hands. They are long-term follow-up experiences. They teach us to be human.

Doctors, trained to accept blood and other body fluids as all in a day's work, are not trained to clean up poop or wipe up vomit; having a child is, among other things, a very long tutorial in how to do exactly those things. And that changes the way you feel about taking care of patients and your ability to stay removed from certain biological and emotional realities as you walk your heroic path.

Does all this apply to men as well as women? Probably; there may still be men in this world who have babies but are unable (read: unwilling) to change diapers, but even they open up huge windows in their self-defenses when they love their children. Nowadays, many men—even men who work medical hours—are at least semicompetent when it comes to child care and have some appreciation for the rewards and the difficulties of day-to-day duties. And they understand, perhaps, that never being there means losing out on something besides a lot of dirty diapers.

So childbearing can be the way we learn about being patients, and raising children can be the way we learn about being human. Medical education can crowd a lot out of your life and can leave you with awesome human responsibilities at a callow and over-educated early age. Children are a crash course (though not a short one) in everything that medical training leaves out.

> *It isn't like I said,* I want to go into medicine, should I have kids? *I thought,* I definitely want to have a family—should I or should I not go into medicine?
>
> *I don't want to be as dogmatic as my father was. When we were young he was experiencing lots of pressure starting up his own practice, and he would come home and take it out on us.*
> —Research assistant, age 30

Having a child is also a tutorial in making mistakes, in finding ways to accept your own fallibility—yet finding some real authority for yourself amidst your weaknesses and inconsistencies. Doctors, as parents and as professionals, do not necessarily react well when their authority is challenged. Their families may find themselves laboring under the yoke of the doctor parent's dual authority. The expertise and manner of decisive command acquired through years of training and reinforcement are not easily shed at home.

In *The Group*, McCarthy delineates, with her usual satiric eye, the conflicts within Priss as she considers her husband the expert. "She had begun to see that she might have to defend Stephen against Sloan, and the more so because Sloan was a doctor and therefore had a double authority. She found that she was checking what Sloan said against what the nurses said, against what the Department of Labor pamphlet said, against *Parents' Magazine*. . . . There was a side of Sloan, she had decided, that she mistrusted, a side that could be summed up by saying that he was a Republican. . . . She did not like the thought of a Republican controlling the destiny of a helpless baby. In medicine, Sloan was quite forward-looking, but he was enamored of his own theories, which he wanted to enforce, like Prohibition, regardless of the human factor. She wondered, really, whether he was going to make a very good pediatrician." First, of course, she had begun to doubt whether he would make a very good father. By assuming the cloak of "double authority," Stephen made it impossible for his wife to believe in one without the other.

Many of us, as physicians, have seen our doctorly authority undermined when our children refuse to follow our developmental predictions or when their illnesses fail to cooperate with our diagnoses. On a family trip to Denmark once, I decided my 3-year-old son was developing a periorbital cellulitis and explained to his terrified father that he would need to be admitted to a hospital and treated with IV antibiotics. After the Danish doctor reassured me that what Benjamin really had was a bug bite and a swollen eyelid, I found myself trying to expound this new diagnosis with equal certainty. And then there was the time Benjamin had a fever in India and I diagnosed probable typhoid—it turned out to be an ear infection. Mind you, I'm a pediatrician; I see children with fevers constantly, and I don't tend to get ear infections and typhoid confused. I'm just not a very good pediatrician when my anxieties about my own children get in the way.

As physicians, we may use our medical knowledge to protect our children; we may bring our training to bear on the various issues of growth, development, infection, and injury that come up in daily life with children. But at the same time, we feel the same anxiety and pain our patients and their families feel when something is going wrong; we have all the knowledge and yet we are without the defenses we learned along with that knowledge.

When my daughter was born it was spring, then summer. She would sweat, and I would taste her sweat, and I was convinced she had

Powerful Innovators

Next to excellence is the appreciation of it.

William Makepeace Thackeray

Miles is pleased to sponsor this series on Powerful Innovators to remember, recognize, and appreciate the truly remarkable achievements of the best of the medical profession.

We salute these individuals; we applaud their efforts; we remember their deeds.

More importantly, we salute and applaud the efforts today's physicians make every day.

H. Brian Allen, MD, FFPM
Director, Scientific Relations
Miles Inc.
Pharmaceutical Division

Powerful
Numbers
speak for themselves:

*2 ...The number of hours ciprofloxacin
needed for complete killing* in vitro *of
a representative isolate of* Pseudomonas
aeruginosa, *a rate that was more than
two times faster than that of ceftazidime,
piperacillin, imipenem, or tobramycin.**

*4 ...The number of stages of cell growth
during which ciprofloxacin actively kills—
the lag, exponential growth, stationary, and
dying-off phases.**

*96 ...The percent susceptibility of 71,389
clinical isolates of Enterobacteriaceae to
ciprofloxacin.**

The most potent fluoroquinolone.[1-3]*

In vitro activity does not necessarily imply a correlation with *in vivo* results.

See complete prescribing information at the end of this book.

Miles Inc.
Pharmaceutical Division
400 Morgan Lane
West Haven, CT 06516

*cystic fibrosis. I knew that was ridiculous, and I didn't mention it
to anyone for weeks. Then finally I mentioned it to my wife, and
she proceeded to laugh me out of existence.*

*Then when my daughter was a month and a half old, she would
not pull to sit, she would just pull up to a stand. Her little, rigid
body would stand there, and I was sure she had cerebral palsy, and
once again I didn't tell anyone. I don't know; if my wife wasn't a
doctor, would she have taken me more seriously? If I'd been married to anyone who wasn't overwhelmingly sane, she might have
been taken in.*

—Pediatrician, age 32

Sometimes it can be reassuring to know a little bit more than
other parents, but sometimes it is completely terrifying. Either
way, children inevitably teach us all the lessons we may never have
wanted to learn about the preciousness of good health and the
precariousness of good fortune.

*Dad always hoped one of us would go into medicine, but he never
pushed us, and one by one we didn't. We all started out majoring
in biology—it wasn't till later that I thought about medical school,
when I realized I didn't want to go on and get a graduate degree
in biology. I thought about how he was always on call. I had to seriously ask myself if I wanted to live a life like that. I realized that,
yeah, I'd be willing to make that sacrifice. And then there was the
intellectual aspect of what he did—he really seemed to enjoy learning more. He went to medical school in the '40s, and a lot of what
I learned in college he didn't know, and he seemed to enjoy learning it.*

*I liked the way people put trust in him, looked up to him. I re-
member being in his office, hearing him talk to several patients and
some people we knew as friends, and how they seemed to confide in
him about problems other than medical problems. I could see myself in that role; with my friends, I'm the one they can talk to, I'm
nonjudgmental. I saw that in the way he dealt with people.*

—Research assistant, age 30

For a group of parents who according to all their children are
not around nearly enough, physicians seem to do a very good job
of communicating the satisfaction they take in their jobs and the
meaning they find in their lives. Most of the doctors' children I
spoke to had a strong sense of why their parents were doing the

jobs they did. This is most vividly expressed by those children who chose to go into medicine themselves, accepting the vicissitudes of a medical life with the special authority of those who know it from the inside out.

There was never any pressure on me except to do well in school. His only qualification about what I did was he didn't want me to be either a psychiatrist or a radiologist—he felt it wasn't worth spending all that money and then not becoming a doctor. In some respects I'm creating a similar life, though I'm doing more bench research. I knew more about academic medicine than private practice. I had a sense that he enjoys what he's doing, it's not just a job, that it's incredibly fulfilling and meaningful. I think he would be happy to be a country doctor in Appalachia.

—Internist, age 33

It is certainly possible to dwell on the difficulties of combining children and a career in medicine—especially for women—and easy to look to the medical literature for evidence that many physicians find themselves in troubled marriages and lives damaged by stress and substance abuse. But it is also worth looking at the satisfactions of this balancing act. In 1987, Dalia G. Ducker questioned a group of female physicians and found that her subjects described a high level of both personal and professional satisfaction.

Lillian Kaufman Cartwright, in her *JAMWA* article "Role Montage: Life Patterns of Professional Women," offered an analogy for the ways that physicians put their lives together from pieces that do not easily fit. She wrote: "Collage, montage, or three-dimensional assemblage are not to be viewed as trivial art forms but the best and most appropriate we can hope for given the schisms, pluralism, disjunctions, and ironic juxtapositions of contemporary life. Coherent formal synthesis relies on a single, more stable society or an observer who is an idealist, not especially perceptive, or hopelessly enraptured with the fictitious." It's not always easy to persuade yourself that such a life is nevertheless a work of art. Imagine a collage where the paper keeps sliding and the glue doesn't always stick, with pieces pasted on top of other pieces, some important ones that keep falling off, blank spaces where no images will adhere, and dense patches that look like a rat's nest of bits and scraps. This is your life (or perhaps just your living room): is it a work of art, or is it just a mess?

Still, I find it an encouraging metaphor, a useful image for the combination of many elements, each worth cherishing but none easily compatible with any of the others. And if, as you stare at this montage, you begin to see reflections of one element in the texture of another, then perhaps you may find harmonies in your life that do not depend on a deluded determination to achieve a single, coherent synthesis.

> *Well, it really depends on what kind of doctor your parent is. Sometimes it can be not so fun, like when your mother has to go on call. Sometimes it can be fun, like when you go to visit the hospital and you know the doctors. And once in a while you'll get an unsuspected treat, like a nice snack from the hospital cafeteria.*
> —Benjamin, age 7

It is worthwhile, the struggle to be a good doctor. It is also an essential endeavor to do a good job with your children. Having children may make you a better doctor; it may advance your education in what it means to be a human being. It will certainly make you a more frazzled doctor. You will be the parent you are in part because you are a doctor, and you will be the doctor you are in part because of your children. Your medical career will shape their childhood years, and they, in return, will shape you as a physician.

ADDITIONAL COPIES

To order copies of *Taking Care of Your Own* for friends or colleagues, please write to The Grand Rounds Press, Whittle Books, 333 Main St., Knoxville, Tenn. 37902. Please include the recipient's name, mailing address, and, where applicable, primary specialty and ME number.

For a single copy, please enclose a check for $21.95 plus $1.50 for postage and handling, payable to The Grand Rounds Press. Quantities may be limited. Discounts apply to bulk orders when available. For more information about The Grand Rounds Press, please call 800-765-5889.

Also available, at the same price, are copies of the previous books from The Grand Rounds Press:

The Doctor Watchers by Spencer Vibbert
The New Genetics by Leon Jaroff
Surgeon Koop by Gregg Easterbrook
Inside Medical Washington by James H. Sammons, M.D.
Medicine For Sale by Richard Currey
The Doctor Dilemma by Gerald R. Weissmann, M.D.

Please allow four weeks for delivery.
Tennessee residents must add 8¼ percent sales tax.

PRESCRIBING INFORMATION
APPENDIX

CIPRO® I.V.
(ciprofloxacin)
For Intravenous Infusion

PZ100736

DESCRIPTION

Cipro® I.V. (ciprofloxacin) is a synthetic broad-spectrum antimicrobial agent for intravenous (iv) administration. Ciprofloxacin, a fluoroquinolone, is 1-cyclo-propyl-6-fluoro-1, 4-dihydro-4-oxo-7-(1-piperazinyl)-3-quinolinecarboxylic acid. Its empirical formula is $C_{17}H_{18}FN_3O_3$ and its chemical structure is:

Ciprofloxacin is a faint to light yellow crystalline powder with a molecular weight of 331.4. It is soluble in dilute (0.1N) hydrochloric acid and is practically insoluble in water and ethanol. Ciprofloxacin differs from other quinolones in that it has a fluorine atom at the 6-position, a piperazine moiety at the 7-position, and a cyclo-propyl ring at the 1-position. Cipro® I.V. solutions are available as 1.0% aqueous concentrates, which are intended for dilution prior to administration, and as a 0.2% ready-for-use infusion solution in 5% Dextrose Injection. All formulas contain lactic acid as a solubilizing agent and hydrochloric acid for pH adjustment. The pH range for the 1.0% aqueous concentrates in vials is 3.3 to 3.9. The pH range for the 0.2% ready-for-use infusion solutions is 3.5 to 4.6.

The plastic container is fabricated from a specially formulated polyvinyl chloride. Solutions in contact with the plastic container can leach out certain of its chemical components in very small amounts within the expiration period, e.g., di(2-ethyl-hexyl) phthalate (DEHP), up to 5 parts per million. The suitability of the plastic has been confirmed in tests in animals according to USP biological tests for plastic containers as well as by tissue culture toxicity studies.

CLINICAL PHARMACOLOGY

Following 60-minute intravenous infusions of 200 mg and 400 mg ciprofloxacin to normal volunteers, the mean maximum serum concentrations achieved were 2.1 and 4.6 µg/mL, respectively; the concentrations at 12 hours were 0.1 and 0.2 µg/mL, respectively.

Steady-state Ciprofloxacin Serum Concentrations (µg/mL) After 60-minute IV Infusions q 12 h.

Dose	30 min.	1 hr	3 hr	6 hr	8 hr	12 hr
			Time after starting the infusion			
200 mg	1.7	2.1	0.6	0.3	0.2	0.1
400 mg	3.7	4.6	1.3	0.7	0.5	0.2

The pharmacokinetics of ciprofloxacin are linear over the dose range of 200 to 400 mg administered intravenously. The serum elimination half-life is approximately 5–6 hours and the total clearance is around 35 L/hr. Comparison of the pharmacokinetic parameters following the 1st and 5th iv dose on a q 12 h regimen indicates no evidence of drug accumulation.

The absolute bioavailability of oral ciprofloxacin is within a range of 70–80% with no substantial loss by first pass metabolism. An intravenous infusion of 400 mg ciprofloxacin given over 60 minutes every 12 hours has been shown to produce an area under the serum concentration time curve (AUC) equivalent to that produced by a 500 mg oral dose given every 12 hours. A 400 mg iv dose administered over 60 minutes every 12 hours results in a C_{max} similar to that observed with a 750 mg oral dose. An infusion of 200 mg ciprofloxacin given every 12 hours produces an AUC equivalent to that produced by a 250 mg oral dose given every 12 hours.

After intravenous administration, approximately 50% to 70% of the dose is excreted in the urine as unchanged drug. Following a 200 mg iv dose, concentrations in the urine usually exceed 200 µg/mL 0–2 hours after dosing and are generally greater than 15 µg/mL 8–12 hours after dosing. Following a 400 mg iv dose, urine concentrations generally exceed 400 µg/mL 0–2 hours after dosing and are usually greater than 30 µg/mL 8–12 hours after dosing. The renal clearance is approximately 22 L/hr. The urinary excretion of ciprofloxacin is virtually complete by 24 hours after dosing.

Co-administration of probenecid with ciprofloxacin results in about a 50% reduction in the ciprofloxacin renal clearance and a 50% increase in its concentration in the systemic circulation. Although bile concentrations of ciprofloxacin are several-fold higher than serum concentrations after intravenous dosing, only a small amount of the administered dose (<1%) is recovered from the bile as unchanged drug. Approximately 15% of an iv dose is recovered from the feces within 5 days after dosing.

After iv administration, three metabolites of ciprofloxacin have been identified in human urine which together account for approximately 10% of the intravenous dose.

In patients with reduced renal function, the half-life of ciprofloxacin is slightly prolonged and dosage adjustments may be required. (See DOSAGE AND ADMINISTRATION.)

In preliminary studies in patients with stable chronic liver cirrhosis, no significant changes in ciprofloxacin pharmacokinetics have been observed. However, the kinetics of ciprofloxacin in patients with acute hepatic insufficiency have not been fully elucidated.

The binding of ciprofloxacin to serum proteins is 20 to 40%.

After intravenous administration, ciprofloxacin is present in saliva, nasal and bronchial secretions, sputum, skin blister fluid, lymph, peritoneal fluid, bile and prostatic secretions. It has also been detected in the lung, skin, fat, muscle, cartilage and bone. Although the drug diffuses into cerebrospinal fluid (CSF), CSF concentrations are generally less than 10% of peak serum concentrations. Levels of the drug in the aqueous and vitreous chambers of the eye are lower than in serum.

Microbiology: Ciprofloxacin has *in vitro* activity against a wide range of gram-negative and gram-positive organisms. The bactericidal action of ciprofloxacin results from interference with the enzyme DNA gyrase which is needed for the synthesis of bacterial DNA.

Ciprofloxacin has been shown to be active against most strains of the following organisms both *in vitro* and in clinical infections. (See INDICATIONS AND USAGE section.)

Gram-positive bacteria
Enterococcus faecalis (Many strains are only moderately susceptible)
Staphylococcus aureus
Staphylococcus epidermidis
Streptococcus pneumoniae
Streptococcus pyogenes

Gram-negative bacteria
Citrobacter diversus
Citrobacter freundii
Enterobacter cloacae
Escherichia coli
Haemophilus influenzae
Haemophilus parainfluenzae
Klebsiella pneumoniae

Morganella morganii
Proteus mirabilis
Proteus vulgaris
Providencia rettgeri
Providencia stuartii
Pseudomonas aeruginosa
Serratia marcescens

Ciprofloxacin has been shown to be active *in vitro* against most strains of the following organisms; however, *the clinical significance of these data is unknown.*

Gram-positive bacteria
Staphylococcus haemolyticus
Staphylococcus hominis
Staphylococcus saprophyticus

Gram-negative bacteria
Acinetobacter calcoaceticus
Aeromonas caviae
Aeromonas hydrophila
Brucella melitensis
Campylobacter coli
Campylobacter jejuni
Edwardsiella tarda
Enterobacter aerogenes
Haemophilus ducreyi
Klebsiella oxytoca
Legionella pneumophila
Moraxella (Branhamella) catarrhalis

Neisseria gonorrhoeae
Neisseria meningitidis
Pasteurella multocida
Salmonella enteritidis
Salmonella typhi
Shigella flexneri
Shigella sonnei
Vibrio cholerae
Vibrio parahaemolyticus
Vibrio vulnificus
Yersinia enterocolitica

Other organisms
Chlamydia trachomatis (only moderately susceptible)
Mycobacterium tuberculosis (only moderately susceptible)

Most strains of *Pseudomonas cepacia* and some strains of *Pseudomonas maltophilia* are resistant to ciprofloxacin as are most anaerobic bacteria, including *Bacteroides fragilis* and *Clostridium difficile*.

Ciprofloxacin is slightly less active when tested at acidic pH. The inoculum size has little effect when tested *in vitro*. The minimum bactericidal concentration (MBC) generally does not exceed the minimum inhibitory concentration (MIC) by more than a factor of 2. Resistance to ciprofloxacin *in vitro* usually develops slowly (multiple-step mutation).

Ciprofloxacin does not cross-react with other antimicrobial agents such as beta-lactams or aminoglycosides; therefore, organisms resistant to these drugs may be susceptible to ciprofloxacin.

In vitro studies have shown that additive activity often results when ciprofloxacin is combined with other antimicrobial agents such as beta-lactams, aminoglycosides, clindamycin, or metronidazole. Synergy has been reported particularly with the combination of ciprofloxacin and a beta-lactam; antagonism is observed only rarely.

Susceptibility Tests

Diffusion Techniques: Quantitative methods that require measurement of zone diameters give the most precise estimates of antibiotic susceptibility. One such procedure recommended for use with the 5-µg ciprofloxacin disk is the National Committee for Clinical Laboratory Standards (NCCLS) approved procedure (M2-A4--Performance Standards for Antimicrobial Disc Susceptibility Tests 1990). Only a 5-µg ciprofloxacin disk should be used, and it should not be used for testing susceptibility to less quinolones; there are no suitable surrogate disks.

Results of laboratory tests using 5-µg ciprofloxacin disks should be interpreted using the following criteria:

Zone Diameter (mm)		Interpretation
≥ 21	(S)	Susceptible
16 - 20	(MS)	Moderately Susceptible
≤ 15	(R)	Resistant

Dilution Techniques: Broth and agar dilution methods, such as those recommended by the NCCLS (M7-A2--Methods for Dilution Antimicrobial Susceptibility Tests for Bacteria that Grow Aerobically 1990), may be used to determine the minimum inhibitory concentration (MIC) of ciprofloxacin. MIC test results should be interpreted according to the following criteria:

MIC (µg/mL)		Interpretation
≤ 1	(S)	Susceptible
2	(MS)	Moderately Susceptible
≥ 4	(R)	Resistant

For any susceptibility test, a report of "susceptible" indicates that the pathogen is likely to be inhibited by generally achievable blood levels. A report of "resistant" indicates that the pathogen is not likely to respond. A report of "moderately susceptible" indicates that the pathogen is expected to be susceptible to ciprofloxacin if high doses are used, or if the infection is confined to tissues and fluids in which high ciprofloxacin levels are attained.

The Quality Control (QC) strains should have the following assigned daily ranges for ciprofloxacin.

QC Strains	Disk Zone Diameter (mm)	MIC (µg/mL)
S. aureus (ATCC 25923)	22 – 30	——
S. aureus (ATCC 29213)	——	0.12 – 0.5
E. coli (ATCC 25922)	30 – 40	0.004 – 0.015
P. aeruginosa (ATCC 27853)	25 – 33	0.25 – 1.0
E. faecalis (ATCC 29212)	——	0.25 – 2.0

INDICATIONS AND USAGE

Cipro® I.V. is indicated for the treatment of infections caused by susceptible strains of the designated microorganisms in the conditions listed below when the intravenous administration offers a route of administration advantageous to the patient:

Urinary Tract Infections – mild, moderate, severe and complicated infections caused by *Escherichia coli*, (including cases with secondary bacteremia), *Klebsiella pneumoniae* subspecies *pneumoniae*, *Enterobacter cloacae*, *Serratia marcescens*, *Proteus mirabilis*, *Providencia rettgeri*, *Morganella morganii*, *Citrobacter diversus*, *Citrobacter freundii*, *Pseudomonas aeruginosa*, *Staphylococcus epidermidis*, and *Enterococcus faecalis*.

Cipro® I.V. is also indicated for the treatment of mild to moderate lower respiratory tract infections, skin and skin structure infections and bone and joint infections due to the organisms listed in each section below. In severe and complicated lower respiratory tract infections, skin and skin structure infections and bone and joint infections, safety and effectiveness of the iv formulation have not been established.

Lower Respiratory Infections – mild to moderate infections caused by *Escherichia coli*, *Klebsiella pneumoniae* subspecies *pneumoniae*, *Enterobacter cloacae*, *Proteus mirabilis*, *Pseudomonas aeruginosa*, *Haemophilus influenzae*, *Haemophilus parainfluenzae*, and *Streptococcus pneumoniae*.

Skin and Skin Structure Infections – mild to moderate infections caused by *Escherichia coli*, *Klebsiella pneumoniae* subspecies *pneumoniae*, *Enterobacter cloacae*, *Proteus mirabilis*, *Proteus vulgaris*, *Providencia stuartii*, *Morganella morganii*, *Citrobacter freundii*, *Pseudomonas aeruginosa*, *Staphylococcus aureus*, *Staphylococcus epidermidis*, and *Streptococcus pyogenes*.

Bone and Joint Infections – mild to moderate infections caused by *Enterobacter cloacae*, *Serratia marcescens*, and *Pseudomonas aeruginosa*.

If anaerobic organisms are suspected of contributing to the infection, appropriate therapy should be administered.

Appropriate culture and susceptibility tests should be performed before treatment in order to isolate and identify organisms causing infection and to determine their susceptibility to ciprofloxacin. Therapy with Cipro® I.V. may be initiated before results of these tests are known; once results become available, appropriate therapy should be continued.

As with other drugs, some strains of *Pseudomonas aeruginosa* may develop resistance fairly rapidly during treatment with ciprofloxacin. Culture and susceptibility testing performed periodically during therapy will provide information not only on the therapeutic effect of the antimicrobial agent but also on the possible emergence of bacterial resistance.

CONTRAINDICATIONS

Cipro® I.V. (ciprofloxacin) is contraindicated in persons with a history of hypersensitivity to ciprofloxacin or any member of the quinolone class of antimicrobial agents.

WARNINGS

THE SAFETY AND EFFECTIVENESS OF CIPROFLOXACIN IN CHILDREN, ADOLESCENTS (LESS THAN 18 YEARS OF AGE), PREGNANT WOMEN, AND LACTATING WOMEN HAVE NOT BEEN ESTABLISHED. (SEE PRECAUTIONS - PEDIATRIC USE, PREGNANCY AND NURSING MOTHERS SUBSECTIONS.) Ciprofloxacin causes lameness in immature dogs. Histopathological examination of the weight-bearing joints of these dogs revealed permanent lesions of the cartilage. Related quinolone-class drugs also produce erosions of cartilage of weight-bearing joints and other signs of arthropathy in immature animals of various species. (See ANIMAL PHARMACOLOGY.)

Convulsions have been reported in patients receiving ciprofloxacin. Convulsions, increased intracranial pressure, and toxic psychosis have been reported in patients receiving ciprofloxacin and other drugs of this class. Quinolones may also cause central nervous system (CNS) stimulation which may lead to tremors, restlessness, lightheadedness, confusion and hallucinations. If these reactions occur in patients receiving ciprofloxacin, the drug should be discontinued and appropriate measures instituted. As with all quinolones, ciprofloxacin should be used with caution in patients with known or suspected CNS disorders, such as severe cerebral arteriosclerosis, epilepsy, and other factors that predispose to seizures. (See ADVERSE REACTIONS.)

SERIOUS AND FATAL REACTIONS HAVE BEEN REPORTED IN PATIENTS RECEIVING CONCURRENT ADMINISTRATION OF INTRAVENOUS CIPROFLOXACIN AND THEOPHYLLINE. These reactions have included cardiac arrest, seizure, status epilepticus and respiratory failure. Although similar serious adverse events have been reported in patients receiving theophylline alone, the possibility that these reactions may be potentiated by ciprofloxacin cannot be eliminated. If concomitant use cannot be avoided, serum levels of theophylline should be monitored and dosage adjustments made as appropriate.

Serious and occasionally fatal hypersensitivity (anaphylactic) reactions, some following the first dose, have been reported in patients receiving quinolone therapy. Some reactions were accompanied by cardiovascular collapse, loss of consciousness, tingling, pharyngeal or facial edema, dyspnea, urticaria, and itching. Only a few patients had a history of hypersensitivity reactions. Serious anaphylactic reactions require immediate emergency treatment with epinephrine and other resuscitation measures, including oxygen, intravenous fluids, intravenous antihistamines, corticosteroids, pressor amines and airway management, as clinically indicated.

Severe hypersensitivity reactions characterized by rash, fever, eosinophilia, jaundice, and hepatic necrosis with fatal outcome have also been reported extremely rarely in patients receiving ciprofloxacin along with other drugs. The possibility that these reactions were related to ciprofloxacin cannot be excluded. Ciprofloxacin should be discontinued at the first appearance of a skin rash or any other sign of hypersensitivity.

Pseudomembranous colitis has been reported with nearly all antibacterial agents, including ciprofloxacin, and may range in severity from mild to life-threatening. Therefore, it is important to consider this diagnosis in patients who present with diarrhea subsequent to the administration of antibacterial agents.

Treatment with antibacterial agents alters the normal flora of the colon and may permit overgrowth of clostridia. Studies indicate that a toxin produced by *Clostridium difficile* is one primary cause of "antibiotic-associated colitis".

After the diagnosis of pseudomembranous colitis has been established, therapeutic measures should be initiated. Mild cases of pseudomembranous colitis usually respond to drug discontinuation alone. In moderate to severe cases, consideration should be given to management with fluids and electrolytes, protein supplementation and treatment with an antibacterial drug effective against *C. difficile*.

PRECAUTIONS

General: INTRAVENOUS CIPROFLOXACIN SHOULD BE ADMINISTERED BY SLOW INFUSION OVER A PERIOD OF 60 MINUTES. Local iv site reactions have been reported with the intravenous administration of ciprofloxacin. These reactions are more frequent if infusion time is 30 minutes or less or if small veins of the hand are used. (See ADVERSE REACTIONS.)

Crystals of ciprofloxacin have been observed rarely in the urine of human subjects but more frequently in the urine of laboratory animals, which is usually alkaline. (See ANIMAL PHARMACOLOGY.) Crystalluria related to ciprofloxacin has been reported only rarely in humans because human urine is usually acidic. Alkalinity of the urine should be avoided in patients receiving ciprofloxacin. Patients should be well hydrated to prevent the formation of highly concentrated urine.

Alteration of the dosage regimen is necessary for patients with impairment of renal function. (See DOSAGE AND ADMINISTRATION.)

Moderate to severe phototoxicity manifested by an exaggerated sunburn reaction has been observed in some patients who were exposed to direct sunlight while receiving some members of the quinolone class of drugs. Excessive sunlight should be avoided.

As with any potent drug, periodic assessment of organ system functions, including renal, hepatic, and hematopoietic, is advisable during prolonged therapy.

Information for Patients: Patients should be advised that ciprofloxacin may be associated with hypersensitivity reactions, even following a single dose, and to discontinue the drug at the first sign of a skin rash or other allergic reaction.

Ciprofloxacin may cause dizziness and lightheadedness; therefore, patients should know how they react to this drug before they operate an automobile or machinery or engage in activities requiring mental alertness or coordination.

Patients should be advised that ciprofloxacin may increase the effects of theophylline and caffeine. There is a possibility of caffeine accumulation when products containing caffeine are consumed while taking quinolones.

Drug Interactions: As with other quinolones, concurrent administration of ciprofloxacin with theophylline may lead to elevated serum concentrations of theophylline and prolongation of its elimination half-life. This may result in increased risk of theophylline-related adverse reactions. (See WARNINGS.) If concomitant use cannot be avoided, serum levels of theophylline should be monitored and dosage adjustments made as appropriate.

Some quinolones, including ciprofloxacin, have also been shown to interfere with the metabolism of caffeine. This may lead to reduced clearance of caffeine and a prolongation of its serum half-life.

Some quinolones, including ciprofloxacin, have been associated with transient elevations in serum creatinine in patients receiving cyclosporine concomitantly.

Quinolones have been reported to enhance the effects of the oral anticoagulant warfarin or its derivatives. When these products are administered concomitantly, prothrombin time or other suitable coagulation tests should be closely monitored.

Probenecid interferes with renal tubular secretion of ciprofloxacin and produces an increase in the level of ciprofloxacin in the serum. This should be considered if patients are receiving both drugs concomitantly.

As with other broad-spectrum antimicrobial agents, prolonged use of ciprofloxacin may result in overgrowth of nonsusceptible organisms. Repeated evaluation of the patient's condition and microbial susceptibility testing are essential. If superinfection occurs during therapy, appropriate measures should be taken.

Carcinogenesis, Mutagenesis, Impairment of Fertility: Eight *in vitro* mutagenicity tests have been conducted with ciprofloxacin. Test results are listed below:

Salmonella/Microsome Test (Negative)
E. coli DNA Repair Assay (Negative)
Mouse Lymphoma Cell Forward Mutation Assay (Positive)
Chinese Hamster V_{79} Cell HGPRT Test (Negative)
Syrian Hamster Embryo Cell Transformation Assay (Negative)
Saccharomyces cerevisiae Point Mutation Assay (Negative)
Saccharomyces cerevisiae Mitotic Crossover and Gene Conversion Assay (Negative)
Rat Hepatocyte DNA Repair Assay (Positive)

Thus, two of the eight tests were positive, but results of the following three *in vivo* test systems gave negative results:

Rat Hepatocyte DNA Repair Assay
Micronucleus Test (Mice)
Dominant Lethal Test (Mice)

Long-term carcinogenicity studies in mice and rats have been completed. After daily oral dosing for up to 2 years, there is no evidence that ciprofloxacin has any carcinogenic or tumorigenic effects in these species.

Pregnancy: Teratogenic Effects. Pregnancy Category C: Reproduction studies have been performed in rats and mice at doses up to 6 times the usual daily human dose and have revealed no evidence of impaired fertility or harm to the fetus due to ciprofloxacin. In rabbits, ciprofloxacin (30 and 100 mg/kg orally) produced gastrointestinal disturbances resulting in maternal weight loss and an increased incidence of abortion. No teratogenicity was observed at either dose. After intravenous administration of doses up to 20 mg/kg, no maternal toxicity was produced, and no embryotoxicity or teratogenicity was observed. There are, however, no adequate and well-controlled studies in pregnant women. Ciprofloxacin should be used during pregnancy only if the potential benefit justifies the potential risk to the fetus. (See WARNINGS.)

Nursing Mothers: Ciprofloxacin is excreted in human milk. Because of the potential for serious adverse reactions in infants nursing from mothers taking ciprofloxacin, a decision should be made either to discontinue nursing or to discontinue the drug, taking into account the importance of the drug to the mother.

Pediatric Use: Safety and effectiveness in children and adolescents less than 18 years of age have not been established. Ciprofloxacin causes arthropathy in juvenile animals. (See WARNINGS.)

ADVERSE REACTIONS

The most frequently reported events, without regard to drug relationship, among patients treated with intravenous ciprofloxacin were nausea, diarrhea, central nervous system disturbance, local iv site reactions, abnormalities of liver associated enzymes (hepatic enzymes) and eosinophilia. Headache, restlessness and rash were also noted in greater than 1% of patients treated with the most common doses of ciprofloxacin.

Local iv site reactions have been reported with the intravenous administration of ciprofloxacin. These reactions are more frequent if the infusion time is 30 minutes or less. These may appear as local skin reactions which resolve rapidly upon completion of the infusion. Subsequent intravenous administration is not contraindicated unless the reactions recur or worsen.

Additional events, without regard to drug relationship or route of administration, that occurred in 1% or less of ciprofloxacin courses are listed below:

GASTROINTESTINAL: ileus; jaundice; gastrointestinal bleeding; *C. difficile* associated diarrhea; pseudomembranous colitis; pancreatitis; hepatic necrosis; intestinal perforation; dyspepsia; epigastric or abdominal pain; vomiting; constipation; oral ulceration; oral candidiasis; mouth dryness; anorexia; dysphagia; flatulence.

CENTRAL NERVOUS SYSTEM: convulsive seizures, paranoia, toxic psychosis, depression, dysphasia, phobia, depersonalization, manic reaction, unresponsiveness, ataxia, confusion, hallucinations, dizziness, lightheadedness, paresthesia, anxiety, tremor, insomnia, nightmares, weakness, drowsiness, irritability, malaise, lethargy.

SKIN/HYPERSENSITIVITY: anaphylactic reactions; erythema multiforme/-Stevens-Johnson syndrome; exfoliative dermatitis; toxic epidermal necrolysis; vasculitis; angioedema; edema of the lips, face, neck, conjunctivae, hands or lower extremities; purpura; fever; chills; flushing; pruritus; urticaria; cutaneous candidiasis; vesicles; increased perspiration; hyperpigmentation; erythema nodosum; photosensitivity.

Allergic reactions ranging from urticaria to anaphylactic reactions have been reported. (See WARNINGS.)

SPECIAL SENSES: decreased visual acuity, blurred vision, disturbed vision (flashing lights, change in color perception, overbrightness of lights, diplopia), eye pain, anosmia, hearing loss, tinnitus, nystagmus, a bad taste.

MUSCULOSKELETAL: joint pain; jaw, arm or back pain; joint stiffness; neck and chest pain; achiness; flareup of gout.

RENAL/UROGENITAL: renal failure, interstitial nephritis, hemorrhagic cystitis, renal calculi, frequent urination, acidosis, urethral bleeding, polyuria, urinary retention, gynecomastia, candiduria, vaginitis. Crystalluria, cylindruria, hematuria, and albuminuria have also been reported.

CARDIOVASCULAR: cardiovascular collapse, cardiopulmonary arrest, myocardial infarction, arrhythmia, tachycardia, palpitation, cerebral thrombosis, syncope, cardiac murmur, hypertension, hypotension, angina pectoris.

RESPIRATORY: respiratory arrest, pulmonary embolism, dyspnea, pulmonary edema, respiratory distress, pleural effusion, hemoptysis, epistaxis, hiccough.

IV INFUSION SITE: thrombophlebitis, burning, pain, pruritus, paresthesia, erythema, swelling.

Also reported were agranulocytosis, prolongation of prothrombin time and possible exacerbation of myasthenia gravis.

Many of these events were described as only mild or moderate in severity, abated soon after the drug was discontinued and required no treatment.

In several instances, nausea, vomiting, tremor, irritability or palpitation were judged by investigators to be related to elevated serum levels of theophylline possibly as a result of drug interaction with ciprofloxacin.

Adverse Laboratory Changes: The most frequently reported changes in laboratory parameters with intravenous ciprofloxacin therapy, without regard to drug relationship, were:

Hepatic	—	Elevations of AST (SGOT), ALT (SGPT), alkaline phosphatase, LDH and serum bilirubin.
Hematologic	—	Elevated eosinophil and platelet counts, decreased platelet counts, hemoglobin and/or hematocrit.
Renal	—	Elevations of serum creatinine, BUN, uric acid.
Other	—	Elevations of serum creatine phosphokinase, serum theophylline (in patients receiving theophylline concomitantly), blood glucose, and triglycerides.

Other changes occurring infrequently were: decreased leukocyte count, elevated atypical lymphocyte count, immature WBCs, elevated serum calcium, elevation of serum gamma-glutamyl transpeptidase (γ GT), decreased BUN, decreased uric acid, decreased total serum protein, decreased serum albumin, decreased serum potassium, elevated serum potassium, elevated serum cholesterol.

Other changes occurring rarely during administration of ciprofloxacin were: elevation of serum amylase, decrease of blood glucose, pancytopenia, leukocytosis, elevated sedimentation rate, change in serum phenytoin, decreased prothrombin time, hemolytic anemia, and bleeding diathesis.

OVERDOSAGE

In the event of acute overdosage, the patient should be carefully observed and given supportive treatment. Adequate hydration must be maintained. Only a small amount of ciprofloxacin (<10%) is removed from the body after hemodialysis or peritoneal dialysis.

DOSAGE AND ADMINISTRATION

The recommended adult dosage for urinary tract infections of mild to moderate severity is 200 mg every 12 hours. For severe or complicated urinary tract infections the recommended dosage is 400 mg every 12 hours.

The recommended adult dosage for lower respiratory tract infections, skin and skin structure infections and bone and joint infections of mild to moderate severity is 400 mg every 12 hours.

The determination of dosage for any particular patient must take into consideration the severity and nature of the infection, the susceptibility of the causative organism, the integrity of the patient's host-defense mechanisms and the status of renal and hepatic function.

DOSAGE GUIDELINES

Location of Infection	Type or Severity	Intravenous Unit Dose	Frequency	Daily Dose
Urinary tract	Mild/ Moderate	200 mg	q 12 h	400 mg
	Severe/ Complicated	400 mg	q 12 h	800 mg
Lower Respiratory tract; Skin and Skin Structure; Bone and Joint	Mild/ Moderate	400 mg	q 12 h	800 mg

Cipro® I.V. should be administered by intravenous infusion over a period of 60 minutes.

The duration of treatment depends upon the severity of infection. Generally, ciprofloxacin should be continued for at least 2 days after the signs and symptoms of infection have disappeared. The usual duration is 7 to 14 days. Bone and joint infections may require treatment for 4 to 6 weeks or longer.

Ciprofloxacin hydrochloride tablets (Cipro®) for oral administration are available. Parenteral therapy may be changed to oral Cipro® tablets when the condition warrants, at the discretion of the physician. For complete dosage and administration information, see Cipro® tablet package insert.

Impaired Renal Function: The following table provides dosage guidelines for use in patients with renal impairment; however, monitoring of serum drug levels provides the most reliable basis for dosage adjustment.

RECOMMENDED STARTING AND MAINTENANCE DOSES FOR PATIENTS WITH IMPAIRED RENAL FUNCTION

Creatinine Clearance (mL/min)	Dosage
≥ 30	See usual dosage
5 – 29	200 – 400 mg q 18 – 24 hr

When only the serum creatinine concentration is known, the following formula may be used to estimate creatinine clearance.

$$\text{Men: Creatinine clearance (mL/min)} = \frac{\text{Weight (kg)} \times (140 - \text{age})}{72 \times \text{serum creatinine (mg/dL)}}$$

Women: $0.85 \times$ the value calculated for men.

The serum creatinine should represent a steady state of renal function.

For patients with changing renal function or for patients with renal impairment and hepatic insufficiency, measurement of serum concentrations of ciprofloxacin will provide additional guidance for adjusting dosage.

INTRAVENOUS ADMINISTRATION

Cipro® I.V. should be administered by intravenous infusion over a period of 60 minutes. Slow infusion of a dilute solution into a large vein will minimize patient discomfort and reduce the risk of venous irritation.

Vials (Injection Concentrate): THIS PREPARATION MUST BE DILUTED BEFORE USE. The intravenous dose should be prepared by aseptically withdrawing the appropriate volume of concentrate from the vials of Cipro® I.V. This should be diluted with a suitable intravenous solution to a final concentration of 1–2 mg/mL. (See COMPATIBILITY AND STABILITY.) The resulting solution should be infused over a period of 60 minutes by direct infusion or through a Y-type intravenous infusion set which may already be in place.

If this method or the "piggyback" method of administration is used, it is advisable to discontinue temporarily the administration of any other solutions during the infusion of Cipro® I.V.

Flexible Containers: Cipro® I.V. is also available as a 0.2% premixed solution in 5% dextrose in flexible containers of 100 mL or 200 mL. The solutions in flexible containers may be infused as described above.

COMPATIBILITY AND STABILITY

Ciprofloxacin injection 1% (10 mg/mL), when diluted with the following intravenous solutions to concentrations of 0.5 to 2.0 mg/mL, is stable for up to 14 days at refrigerated or room temperature storage.

0.9% Sodium Chloride Injection, USP
5% Dextrose Injection, USP

If Cipro® I.V. is to be given concomitantly with another drug, each drug should be given separately in accordance with the recommended dosage and route of administration for each drug.

HOW SUPPLIED

Cipro® I.V. (ciprofloxacin) is available as a clear, colorless to slightly yellowish solution. Cipro® I.V. is available in 200 mg and 400 mg strengths. The concentrate is supplied in vials while the premixed solution is supplied in flexible containers as follows:

CONTAINER	SIZE	STRENGTH	NDC NUMBER
Vial:	20mL	200 mg, 1%	0026-8562-20
	40mL	400 mg, 1%	0026-8564-64
Flexible Container:	100mL 5% dextrose	200 mg, 0.2%	0026-8552-36
	200mL 5% dextrose	400 mg, 0.2%	0026-8554-63

STORAGE

Vials:	Store between 41 – 77°F (5 – 25°C).
Flexible Container:	Store between 41 – 77°F (5 – 25°C).

Protect from light, avoid excessive heat, protect from freezing.

Ciprofloxacin is also available as Cipro® (ciprofloxacin HCl) Tablets 250, 500 and 750 mg.

ANIMAL PHARMACOLOGY

Ciprofloxacin and other quinolones have been shown to cause arthropathy in immature animals of most species tested. (See WARNINGS.) Damage of weight-bearing joints was observed in juvenile dogs and rats. In young beagles, 100 mg/kg ciprofloxacin given daily for 4 weeks caused degenerative articular changes of the knee joint. At 30 mg/kg, the effect on the joint was minimal. In a subsequent study in beagles, removal of weight-bearing from the joint reduced the lesions but did not totally prevent them.

Crystalluria, sometimes associated with secondary nephropathy, occurs in laboratory animals dosed with ciprofloxacin. This is primarily related to the reduced solubility of ciprofloxacin under alkaline conditions, which predominate in the urine of test animals; in man, crystalluria is rare since human urine is typically acidic. In rhesus monkeys, crystalluria without nephropathy has been noted after intravenous doses as low as 5 mg/kg. After 6 months of intravenous dosing at 10 mg/kg/day, no nephropathological changes were noted; however, nephropathy was observed after dosing at 20 mg/kg/day for the same duration.

In dogs, ciprofloxacin administered at 3 and 10 mg/kg by rapid intravenous injection (15 sec.) produces pronounced hypotensive effects. These effects are considered to be related to histamine release because they are partially antagonized by pyrilamine, an antihistamine. In rhesus monkeys, rapid intravenous injection also produces hypotension, but the effect in this species is inconsistent and less pronounced.

In mice, concomitant administration of nonsteroidal anti-inflammatory drugs, such as fenbufen, phenylbutazone and indomethacin, with quinolones has been reported to enhance the CNS stimulatory effect of quinolones.

Ocular toxicity, seen with some related drugs, has not been observed in ciprofloxacin-treated animals.

MILES
Miles Inc.
Pharmaceutical Division
400 Morgan Lane
West Haven, CT 06516 USA

Caution: Federal (USA) Law prohibits dispensing without a prescription.

PZ100736 9/91 BAY q 3939 5202-4-A-U.S.-1 1628
06-4745 Printed In U.S.A.

References: **1.** Phillips I, King A. Comparative activity of the 4-quinolones. *Rev Infect Dis.* 1988;10(suppl 1):S70-S76. **2.** Auckenthaler R, Michéa-Hamzehpour M, Pechère JC. *In-vitro* activity of newer quinolones against aerobic bacteria. *J Antimicrob Chemother.* 1986;17(suppl B): 29-39. **3.** Pernet A. Temafloxacin overview. In: *Temafloxacin: A New Standard in Quinolones.* New York, NY: AVMD Group; 1990:1-13.

CIPRO®
(ciprofloxacin hydrochloride)
TABLETS

PZ100735

DESCRIPTION

Cipro® (ciprofloxacin hydrochloride) is a synthetic broad spectrum antibacterial agent for oral administration. Ciprofloxacin, a fluoroquinolone, is available as the monohydrochloride monohydrate salt of 1-cyclopropyl-6-fluoro-1, 4-dihydro-4-oxo-7-(1-piperazinyl)-3-quinolinecarboxylic acid. It is a faintly yellowish to light yellow crystalline substance with a molecular weight of 385.8. Its empirical formula is $C_{17}H_{18}FN_3O_3 \cdot HCl \cdot H_2O$ and its chemical structure is as follows:

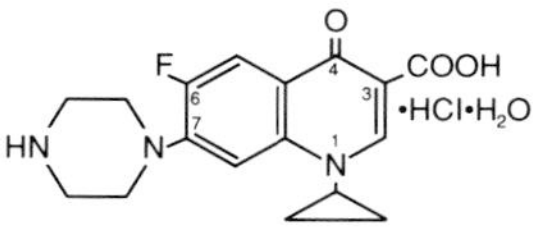

Cipro® is available in 250-mg, 500-mg and 750-mg (ciprofloxacin equivalent) film-coated tablets. The inactive ingredients are starch, microcrystalline cellulose, silicon dioxide, crospovidone, magnesium stearate, hydroxypropyl methylcellulose, titanium dioxide, polyethylene glycol and water. Ciprofloxacin differs from other quinolones in that it has a fluorine atom at the 6-position, a piperazine moiety at the 7-position, and a cyclopropyl ring at the 1-position. Examples of other antibacterial drugs in the quinolone class are nalidixic acid, cinoxacin, and norfloxacin.

CLINICAL PHARMACOLOGY

Cipro® tablets are rapidly and well absorbed from the gastrointestinal tract after oral administration. The absolute bioavailability is approximately 70% with no substantial loss by first pass metabolism. Serum concentrations increase proportionately with the dose as shown:

Dose (mg)	Maximum Serum Concentration (mcg/mL)	Area Under Curve (AUC) (mcg • hr/mL)
250	1.2	4.8
500	2.4	11.6
750	4.3	20.2
1000	5.4	30.8

Maximum serum concentrations are attained 1 to 2 hours after oral dosing. Mean concentrations 12 hours after dosing with 250, 500, or 750 mg are 0.1, 0.2, and 0.4 mcg/mL, respectively. The serum elimination half-life in subjects with normal renal function is approximately 4 hours.

Approximately 40 to 50% of an orally administered dose is excreted in the urine as unchanged drug. After a 250-mg oral dose, urine concentrations of ciprofloxacin usually exceed 200 mcg/mL during the first two hours and are approximately 30 mcg/mL at 8 to 12 hours after dosing. The urinary excretion of ciprofloxacin is virtually complete within 24 hours after dosing. The renal clearance of ciprofloxacin, which is approximately 300 mL/minute, exceeds the normal glomerular filtration rate of 120 mL/minute. Thus, active tubular secretion would seem to play a significant role in its elimination. Co-administration of probenecid with ciprofloxacin results in about a 50% reduction in the ciprofloxacin renal clearance and a 50% increase in its concentration in the systemic circulation. Although bile concentrations of ciprofloxacin are several fold higher than serum concentrations after oral dosing, only a small amount of the dose administered is recovered from the bile as unchanged drug. An additional 1-2% of the dose is recovered from the bile in the form of metabolites. Approximately 20 to 35% of an oral dose is recovered from the feces within 5 days after dosing. This may arise from either biliary clearance or transintestinal elimination. Four metabolites have been identified in human urine which together account for approximately 15% of an oral dose. The metabolites have antimicrobial activity, but are less active than unchanged ciprofloxacin.

When Cipro® is given concomitantly with food, there is a delay in the absorption of the drug, resulting in peak concentrations that are closer to 2 hours after dosing rather than 1 hour. The overall absorption, however, is not substantially affected. Concurrent administration of antacids containing magnesium hydroxide or aluminum hydroxide may reduce the bioavailability of ciprofloxacin by as much as 90% (See Precautions).

Concomitant administration of ciprofloxacin with theophylline decreases the clearance of theophylline resulting in elevated serum theophylline levels, and increased risk of a patient developing CNS or other adverse reactions (See Precautions).

In patients with reduced renal function, the half-life of ciprofloxacin is slightly prolonged. Dosage adjustments may be required (See Dosage and Administration).

In preliminary studies in patients with stable chronic liver cirrhosis, no significant changes in ciprofloxacin pharmacokinetics have been observed. The kinetics of ciprofloxacin in patients with acute hepatic insufficiency, however, have not been fully elucidated.

The binding of ciprofloxacin to serum proteins is 20 to 40% which is not likely to be high enough to cause significant protein binding interactions with other drugs.

After oral administration ciprofloxacin is widely distributed throughout the body. Tissue concentrations often exceed serum concentrations in both men and women, particularly in genital tissue including the prostate. Ciprofloxacin is present in active form in the saliva, nasal and bronchial secretions, sputum, skin blister fluid, lymph, peritoneal fluid, bile and prostatic secretions. Ciprofloxacin has also been detected in lung, skin, fat, muscle, cartilage, and bone. The drug diffuses into the cerebrospinal fluid (CSF); however, CSF concentrations are generally less than 10% of peak serum concentrations. Low levels of the drug have been detected in the aqueous and vitreous humors of the eye.

Microbiology: Ciprofloxacin has *in vitro* activity against a wide range of gram-negative and gram-positive organisms. The bactericidal action of ciprofloxacin results from interference with the enzyme DNA gyrase which is needed for the synthesis of bacterial DNA.

While *in vitro* studies have demonstrated the susceptibility of most strains of the following microorganisms, clinical efficacy for infections other than those included in the Indications and Usage Section has not been documented:

Gram-Negative: *Escherichia coli; Klebsiella pneumoniae; Klebsiella oxytoca; Enterobacter aerogenes; Enterobacter cloacae; Citrobacter diversus; Citrobacter freundii; Edwardsiella tarda; Salmonella enteritidis; Salmonella typhi; Shigella sonnei; Shigella flexneri; Proteus mirabilis; Proteus vulgaris; Providencia stuartii; Providencia rettgeri; Morganella morganii; Serratia marcescens; Yersinia enterocolitica; Pseudomonas aeruginosa; Acinetobacter calcoaceticus* subsp. *lwoffi; Acinetobacter calcoaceticus* subsp. *anitratus; Haemophilus influenzae; Haemophilus parainfluenzae; Haemophilus ducreyi; Neisseria gonorrhoeae; Neisseria meningitidis; Moraxella (Branhamella) catarrhalis; Campylobacter jejuni; Campylobacter coli; Aeromonas hydrophila; Aeromonas caviae; Vibrio cholerae; Vibrio parahaemolyticus; Vibrio vulnificus; Brucella melitensis; Pasteurella multocida; Legionella pneumophila.*

Gram-Positive: *Staphylococcus aureus* (including methicillin-susceptible and methicillin-resistant strains); *Staphylococcus epidermidis; Staphylococcus haemolyticus; Staphylococcus hominis; Staphylococcus saprophyticus; Streptococcus pyogenes; Streptococcus pneumoniae.*

Most strains of streptococci including *Streptococcus faecalis* are only moderately susceptible to ciprofloxacin as are *Mycobacterium tuberculosis* and *Chlamydia trachomatis.*

Most strains of *Pseudomonas cepacia* and some strains of *Pseudomonas maltophilia* are resistant to ciprofloxacin as are most anaerobic bacteria, including *Bacteroides fragilis* and *Clostridium difficile.*

Ciprofloxacin is slightly less active when tested at acidic pH. The inoculum size has little effect when tested *in vitro.* The minimum bactericidal concentration (MBC) generally does not exceed the minimum inhibitory concentration (MIC) by more than a factor of 2. Resistance to ciprofloxacin *in vitro* develops slowly (multiple-step mutation). Rapid one-step development of resistance has not been observed.

Ciprofloxacin does not cross-react with other antimicrobial agents such as beta-lactams or aminoglycosides; therefore, organisms resistant to these drugs may be susceptible to ciprofloxacin.

In vitro studies have shown that additive activity often results when ciprofloxacin is combined with other antimicrobial agents such as beta-lactams, aminoglycosides, clindamycin, or metronidazole; antagonism is observed only rarely.

Susceptibility Tests

Diffusion Techniques: Quantitative methods that require measurement of zone diameters give the most precise estimates of antibiotic susceptibility. One such procedure recommended for use with the 5-mcg ciprofloxacin disk is the National Committee for Clinical Laboratory Standards (NCCLS) approved procedure. Only a 5-mcg ciprofloxacin disk should be used, and it should not be used for testing susceptibility to less active quinolones; there are no suitable surrogate disks.

Results of laboratory tests using 5-mcg ciprofloxacin disks should be interpreted using the following criteria:

Zone Diameter (mm)	Interpretation
≥ 21	(S) Susceptible
16 – 20	(I) Intermediate (Moderately Susceptible)
≤ 15	(R) Resistant

Dilution Techniques: Broth and agar dilution methods, such as those recommended by the NCCLS, may be used to determine the minimum inhibitory concentration (MIC) of ciprofloxacin. MIC test results should be interpreted according to the following criteria:

MIC (mcg/mL)	Interpretation
≤ 1	(S) Susceptible
> 1 – ≤ 2	(I) Intermediate (Moderately Susceptible)
> 2	(R) Resistant

For any susceptibility test, a report of "susceptible" indicates that the pathogen is likely to respond to ciprofloxacin therapy. A report of "resistant" indicates that the pathogen is not likely to respond. A report of "intermediate" (moderately susceptible) indicates that the pathogen is expected to be susceptible to ciprofloxacin if high doses are used, or if the infection is confined to tissues and fluids in which high ciprofloxacin levels are obtained.

The Quality Control strains should have the following assigned daily ranges for ciprofloxacin.

QC Strains	Disk Zone Diameter (mm)	MIC (mcg/mL)
S. aureus (ATCC 25923)	22 – 30	
S. aureus (ATCC 29213)		0.25 – 1.0
E. coli (ATCC 25922)	30 – 40	0.008 – 0.03
P. aeruginosa (ATCC 27853)	25 – 33	0.25 – 1.0

INDICATIONS AND USAGE

Cipro® is indicated for the treatment of infections caused by susceptible strains of the designated microorganisms in the conditions listed below:

Lower Respiratory Infections caused by *Escherichia coli, Klebsiella pneumoniae, Enterobacter cloacae, Proteus mirabilis, Pseudomonas aeruginosa, Haemophilus influenzae, Haemophilus parainfluenzae,* and *Streptococcus pneumoniae.*

Skin and Skin Structure Infections caused by *Escherichia coli, Klebsiella pneumoniae, Enterobacter cloacae, Proteus mirabilis, Proteus vulgaris, Providencia stuartii, Morganella morganii, Citrobacter freundii, Pseudomonas aeruginosa, Staphylococcus aureus, Staphylococcus epidermidis,* and *Streptococcus pyogenes.*

Bone and Joint Infections caused by *Enterobacter cloacae, Serratia marcescens,* and *Pseudomonas aeruginosa.*

Urinary Tract Infections caused by *Escherichia coli, Klebsiella pneumoniae, Enterobacter cloacae, Serratia marcescens, Proteus mirabilis, Providencia rettgeri, Morganella morganii, Citrobacter diversus, Citrobacter freundii, Pseudomonas aeruginosa, Staphylococcus epidermidis,* and *Streptococcus faecalis.*

Infectious Diarrhea caused by *Escherichia coli* (enterotoxigenic strains), *Campylobacter jejuni, Shigella flexneri** and *Shigella sonnei** when antibacterial therapy is indicated.

*Efficacy for this organism in this organ system was studied in fewer than 10 infections.

Appropriate culture and susceptibility tests should be performed before treatment in order to isolate and identify organisms causing infection and to determine their susceptibility to ciprofloxacin. Therapy with Cipro® may be initiated before results of these tests are known; once results become available appropriate therapy should be continued. As with other drugs, some strains of *Pseudomonas aeruginosa* may develop resistance fairly rapidly during treatment with ciprofloxacin. Culture and susceptibility testing performed periodically during therapy will provide information not only on the therapeutic effect of the antimicrobial agent but also on the possible emergence of bacterial resistance.

CONTRAINDICATIONS

A history of hypersensitivity to ciprofloxacin is a contraindication to its use. A history of hypersensitivity to other quinolones may also contraindicate the use of ciprofloxacin.

WARNINGS

THE SAFETY AND EFFECTIVENESS OF CIPROFLOXACIN IN CHILDREN, ADOLESCENTS (LESS THAN 18 YEARS OF AGE), PREGNANT WOMEN, AND LACTATING WOMEN HAVE NOT BEEN ESTABLISHED. (SEE PRECAUTIONS-PEDIATRIC USE, PREGNANCY AND NURSING MOTHERS SUBSECTIONS.) Ciprofloxacin causes lameness in immature dogs. Histopathological examination of the weight-bearing joints of these dogs revealed permanent lesions of the cartilage. Related quinolone-class drugs also produce erosions of cartilage of weight-bearing joints and other signs of arthropathy in immature animals of various species. (See ANIMAL PHARMACOLOGY.)

Convulsions have been reported in patients receiving ciprofloxacin. Convulsions, increased intracranial pressure, and toxic psychosis have been reported in patients receiving ciprofloxacin and other drugs of this class. Quinolones may also cause central nervous system (CNS) stimulation which may lead to tremors, restlessness, lightheadedness, confusion and hallucinations. If these reactions occur in patients receiving ciprofloxacin, the drug should be discontinued and appropriate measures instituted. As with all quinolones, ciprofloxacin should be used with caution in patients with known or suspected CNS disorders, such as severe cerebral arteriosclerosis, epilepsy, and other factors that predispose to seizures. (See ADVERSE REACTIONS.)

SERIOUS AND FATAL REACTIONS HAVE BEEN REPORTED IN PATIENTS RECEIVING CONCURRENT ADMINISTRATION OF CIPROFLOXACIN AND THEOPHYLLINE. These reactions have included cardiac arrest, seizure, status epilepticus and respiratory failure. Although similar serious adverse events have been reported in patients receiving theophylline alone, the possibility that these reactions may be potentiated by ciprofloxacin cannot be eliminated. If concomitant use cannot be avoided, serum levels of theophylline should be monitored and dosage adjustments made as appropriate.

Serious and occasionally fatal hypersensitivity (anaphylactic) reactions, some following the first dose, have been reported in patients receiving quinolone therapy. Some reactions were accompanied by cardiovascular collapse, loss of consciousness, tingling, pharyngeal or facial edema, dyspnea, urticaria, and itching. Only a few patients had a history of hypersensitivity reactions. Serious anaphylactic reactions require immediate emergency treatment with epinephrine and other resuscitation measures, including oxygen, intravenous antihistamines, corticosteroids, pressor amines and airway management, as clinically indicated.

Severe hypersensitivity reactions characterized by rash, fever, eosinophilia, jaundice, and hepatic necrosis with fatal outcome have also been reported extremely rarely in patients receiving ciprofloxacin along with other drugs. The possibility that these reactions were related to ciprofloxacin cannot be excluded. Ciprofloxacin should be discontinued at the first appearance of a skin rash or any other sign of hypersensitivity.

Pseudomembranous colitis has been reported with nearly all antibacterial agents, including ciprofloxacin, and may range in severity from mild to life-threatening. Therefore, it is important to consider this diagnosis in patients who present with diarrhea subsequent to the administration of antibacterial agents.

Treatment with antibacterial agents alters the normal flora of the colon and may permit overgrowth of clostridia. Studies indicate that a toxin produced by *Clostridium difficile* is one primary cause of "antibiotic-associated colitis".

After the diagnosis of pseudomembranous colitis has been established, therapeutic measures should be initiated. Mild cases of pseudomembranous colitis usually respond to drug discontinuation alone. In moderate to severe cases, consideration should be given to management with fluids and electrolytes, protein supplementation and treatment with an antibacterial drug effective against *C. difficile.*

PRECAUTIONS

General: Crystals of ciprofloxacin have been observed rarely in the urine of human subjects but more frequently in the urine of laboratory animals, which is usually alkaline. (See ANIMAL PHARMACOLOGY.) Crystalluria related to ciprofloxacin has been reported only rarely in humans because human urine is usually acidic. Alkalinity of the urine should be avoided in patients receiving ciprofloxacin. Patients should be well hydrated to prevent the formation of highly concentrated urine.

Alteration of the dosage regimen is necessary for patients with impairment of renal function. (See DOSAGE AND ADMINISTRATION.)

Moderate to severe phototoxicity manifested by an exaggerated sunburn reaction has been observed in some patients who were exposed to direct sunlight while receiving some members of the quinolone class of drugs. Excessive sunlight should be avoided.

As with any potent drug, periodic assessment of organ system functions, including renal, hepatic, and hematopoietic, is advisable during prolonged therapy.

Information for Patients: Patients should be advised that ciprofloxacin may be taken with or without meals. The preferred time of dosing is two hours after a meal. Patients should also be advised to drink fluids liberally and not take antacids containing magnesium, aluminum, or calcium, products containing iron, or multivitamins containing zinc. However, usual dietary intake of calcium has not been shown to alter the absorption of ciprofloxacin.

Patients should be advised that ciprofloxacin may be associated with hypersensitivity reactions, even following a single dose, and to discontinue the drug at the first sign of a skin rash or other allergic reaction.

Ciprofloxacin may cause dizziness and lightheadedness; therefore patients should know how they react to this drug before they operate an automobile or machinery or engage in activities requiring mental alertness or coordination.

Patients should be advised that ciprofloxacin may increase the effects of theophylline and caffeine. There is a possibility of caffeine accumulation when products containing caffeine are consumed while taking quinolones.

Drug Interactions: As with other quinolones, concurrent administration of ciprofloxacin with theophylline may lead to elevated serum concentrations of theophylline and prolongation of its elimination half-life. This may result in increased risk of theophylline-related adverse reactions. (See WARNINGS.) If concomitant use cannot be avoided, serum levels of theophylline should be monitored and dosage adjustments made as appropriate.

Some quinolones, including ciprofloxacin, have also been shown to interfere with the metabolism of caffeine. This may lead to reduced clearance of caffeine and a prolongation of its serum half-life.

Concurrent administration of ciprofloxacin with antacids containing magnesium, aluminum, or calcium; with sucralfate or divalent and trivalent cations such as iron may substantially interfere with the absorption of ciprofloxacin, resulting in serum and urine levels considerably lower than desired. To a lesser extent this effect is demonstrated with zinc-containing multivitamins. (See DOSAGE AND ADMINISTRATION for concurrent administration of these agents with ciprofloxacin.)

Some quinolones, including ciprofloxacin, have been associated with transient elevations in serum creatinine in patients receiving cyclosporine concomitantly.

Quinolones have been reported to enhance the effects of the oral anticoagulant warfarin or its derivatives. When these products are administered concomitantly, prothrombin time or other suitable coagulation tests should be closely monitored.

Probenecid interferes with renal tubular secretion of ciprofloxacin and produces an increase in the level of ciprofloxacin in the serum. This should be considered if patients are receiving both drugs concomitantly.

As with other broad spectrum antimicrobial agents, prolonged use of ciprofloxacin may result in overgrowth of nonsusceptible organisms. Repeated evaluation of the patient's condition and microbial susceptibility testing is essential. If superinfection occurs during therapy, appropriate measures should be taken.

Carcinogenesis, Mutagenesis, Impairment of Fertility: Eight *in vitro* mutagenicity tests have been conducted with ciprofloxacin and the test results are listed below:

Salmonella/Microsome Test (Negative)
E. coli DNA Repair Assay (Negative)
Mouse Lymphoma Cell Forward Mutation Assay (Positive)
Chinese Hamster V_{79} Cell HGPRT Test (Negative)
Syrian Hamster Embryo Cell Transformation Assay (Negative)
Saccharomyces cerevisiae Point Mutation Assay (Negative)
Saccharomyces cerevisiae Mitotic Crossover
   and Gene Conversion Assay (Negative)
Rat Hepatocyte DNA Repair Assay (Positive)

Thus 2 of the 8 tests were positive but results of the following 3 *in vivo* test systems gave negative results:

Rat Hepatocyte DNA Repair Assay
Micronucleus Test (Mice)
Dominant Lethal Test (Mice)

Long term carcinogenicity studies in mice and rats have been completed. After daily oral dosing for up to 2 years, there is no evidence that ciprofloxacin had any carcinogenic or tumorigenic effects in these species.

Pregnancy: Teratogenic Effects. Pregnancy Category C: Reproduction studies have been performed in rats and mice at doses up to 6 times the usual daily human dose and have revealed no evidence of impaired fertility or harm to the fetus due to ciprofloxacin. In rabbits, ciprofloxacin (30 and 100 mg/kg orally) produced gastrointestinal disturbances resulting in maternal weight loss and an increased incidence of abortion. No teratogenicity was observed at either dose. After intravenous administration of doses up to 20 mg/kg, no maternal toxicity was produced, and no embryotoxicity or teratogenicity was observed. There are, however, no adequate and well-controlled studies in pregnant women. Ciprofloxacin should be used during pregnancy only if the potential benefit justifies the potential risk to the fetus. (See WARNINGS.)

Nursing Mothers: Ciprofloxacin is excreted in human milk. Because of the potential for serious adverse reactions in infants nursing from mothers taking ciprofloxacin, a decision should be made either to discontinue nursing or to discontinue the drug, taking into account the importance of the drug to the mother.

Pediatric Use: Safety and effectiveness in children and adolescents less than 18 years of age have not been established. Ciprofloxacin causes arthropathy in juvenile animals. (See WARNINGS.)

ADVERSE REACTIONS

During clinical investigation, 2,799 patients received 2,868 courses of the drug. Adverse events that were considered likely to be drug related occurred in 7.3% of courses, possibly related in 9.2%, (total of 16.5% thought to be possibly or probably related to drug therapy), and remotely related in 3.0%. Ciprofloxacin was discontinued because of an adverse event in 3.5% of courses, primarily involving the gastrointestinal system (1.5%), skin (0.6%), and central nervous system (0.4%). Those events typical of quinolones are italicized.

The most frequently reported events, drug related or not, were nausea (5.2%), diarrhea (2.3%), vomiting (2.0%), abdominal pain/discomfort (1.7%), headache (1.2%), restlessness (1.1%), and rash (1.1%).

Additional events that occurred in less than 1% of ciprofloxacin courses are listed below.

GASTROINTESTINAL: *(See above),* painful oral mucosa, oral candidiasis, dysphagia, intestinal perforation, gastrointestinal bleeding.
CENTRAL NERVOUS SYSTEM: *(See above), dizziness, lightheadedness, insomnia, nightmares, hallucinations, manic reaction, irritability, tremor, ataxia, convulsive seizures, lethargy, drowsiness, weakness, malaise, anorexia, phobia, depersonalization, depression, paresthesia, toxic psychosis.*
SKIN/HYPERSENSITIVITY: *(See above), pruritus, urticaria, photosensitivity, flushing, fever, chills, angioedema, edema of the face, neck, lips, conjunctivae or hands;* cutaneous candidiasis, hyperpigmentation, erythema nodosum.
Allergic reactions ranging from urticaria to anaphylactic reactions have been reported (See WARNINGS).
SPECIAL SENSES: *blurred vision, disturbed vision (change in color perception, overbrightness of lights), decreased visual acuity, diplopia, eye pain, tinnitus, hearing loss, bad taste.*
MUSCULOSKELETAL: *joint or back pain, joint stiffness,* achiness, neck or chest pain, flare up of gout.
RENAL/UROGENITAL: *interstitial nephritis, nephritis, renal failure, polyuria, urinary retention, urethral bleeding, vaginitis, acidosis.*
CARDIOVASCULAR: palpitation, atrial flutter, ventricular ectopy, syncope, hypertension, angina pectoris, myocardial infarction, cardiopulmonary arrest, cerebral thrombosis.
RESPIRATORY: epistaxis, laryngeal or pulmonary edema, hiccough, hemoptysis, dyspnea, bronchospasm, pulmonary embolism.
Most of the adverse events reported were described as only mild or moderate in severity, abated soon after the drug was discontinued, and required no treatment.

In several instances nausea, vomiting, tremor, irritability or palpitation were judged by investigators to be related to elevated plasma levels of theophylline possibly as a result of drug interaction with ciprofloxacin.

Other adverse events reported in the postmarketing phase include anaphylactic reactions, erythema multiforme/Stevens-Johnson syndrome, exfoliative dermatitis, toxic epidermal necrolysis, vasculitis, jaundice, hepatic necrosis, postural hypotension, possible exacerbation of myasthenia gravis, anosmia, confusion, dysphasia, nystagmus, pseudomembranous colitis, pancreatitis, dyspepsia, flatulence, and constipation. Also reported were hemolytic anemia; agranulocytosis; elevation of serum triglycerides, serum cholesterol, blood glucose, serum potassium; prolongation of prothrombin time; albuminuria; candiduria, vaginal candidiasis; renal calculi, and change in serum phenytoin (See PRECAUTIONS).

Adverse Laboratory Changes: Changes in laboratory parameters listed as adverse events without regard to drug relationship:

Hepatic — Elevations of: ALT (SGPT) (1.9%), AST (SGOT) (1.7%), Alkaline Phosphatase (0.8%), LDH (0.4%), serum bilirubin (0.3%). Cholestatic jaundice has been reported.

Hematologic — Eosinophilia (0.6%), leukopenia (0.4%), decreased blood platelets (0.1%), elevated blood platelets (0.1%), pancytopenia (0.1%).

Renal — Elevations of: Serum creatinine (1.1%), BUN (0.9%). CRYSTALLURIA, CYLINDRURIA AND HEMATURIA HAVE BEEN REPORTED.

Other changes occurring in less than 0.1% of courses were: Elevation of serum gammaglutamyl transferase, elevation of serum amylase, reduction in blood glucose, elevated uric acid, decrease in hemoglobin, anemia, bleeding diathesis, increase in blood monocytes, leukocytosis.

OVERDOSAGE
In the event of acute overdosage the stomach should be emptied by inducing vomiting or by gastric lavage. The patient should be carefully observed and given supportive treatment. Adequate hydration must be maintained. Only a small amount of ciprofloxacin (<10%) is removed from the body after hemodialysis or peritoneal dialysis.

DOSAGE AND ADMINISTRATION
The usual adult dosage for patients with urinary tract infections is 250 mg every 12 hours. For patients with complicated infections caused by organisms not highly susceptible, 500 mg may be administered every 12 hours.

Lower respiratory tract infections, skin and skin structure infections, and bone and joint infections may be treated with 500 mg every 12 hours. For more severe or complicated infections, a dosage of 750 mg may be given every 12 hours.

The recommended dosage for Infectious Diarrhea is 500 mg every 12 hours.

DOSAGE GUIDELINES

Location of Infection	Type or Severity	Unit Dose	Frequency	Daily Dose
Urinary tract	Mild/Moderate	250 mg	q 12 h	500 mg
	Severe/Complicated	500 mg	q 12 h	1000 mg
Lower respiratory tract;	Mild/Moderate	500 mg	q 12 h	1000 mg
Bone and Joint; Skin or Skin Structure	Severe/Complicated	750 mg	q 12 h	1500 mg
Infectious Diarrhea	Mild/Moderate/Severe	500 mg	q 12 h	1000 mg

The determination of dosage for any particular patient must take into consideration the severity and nature of the infection, the susceptibility of the causative organism, the integrity of the patient's host-defense mechanisms, and the status of renal function.

The duration of treatment depends upon the severity of infection. Generally ciprofloxacin should be continued for at least 2 days after the signs and symptoms of infection have disappeared. The usual duration is 7 to 14 days; however, for severe and complicated infections more prolonged therapy may be required. Bone and joint infections may require treatment for 4 to 6 weeks or longer. Infectious Diarrhea may be treated for 5-7 days.

Impaired Renal Function: Ciprofloxacin is eliminated primarily by renal excretion; however, the drug is also metabolized and partially cleared through the biliary system of the liver and through the intestine. These alternate pathways of drug elimination appear to compensate for the reduced renal excretion in patients with renal impairment. Nonetheless, some modification of dosage is recommended, particularly for patients with severe renal dysfunction. The following table provides dosage guidelines for use in patients with renal impairment; however, monitoring of serum drug levels provides the most reliable basis for dosage adjustment:

RECOMMENDED STARTING AND MAINTENANCE DOSES FOR PATIENTS WITH IMPAIRED RENAL FUNCTION

Creatinine Clearance (mL/min)	Dose
> 50	See Usual Dosage
30 – 50	250 – 500 mg q 12 h
5 – 29	250 – 500 mg q 18 h
Patients on hemodialysis or Peritoneal dialysis	250 – 500 mg q 24 h (after dialysis)

When only the serum creatinine concentration is known, the following formula may be used to estimate creatinine clearance.

$$\text{Men: Creatinine clearance (mL/min)} = \frac{\text{Weight (kg)} \times (140 - \text{age})}{72 \times \text{serum creatinine (mg/dL)}}$$

Women: $0.85 \times$ the value calculated for men.

The serum creatinine should represent a steady state of renal function.

In patients with severe infections and severe renal impairment, a unit dose of 750 mg may be administered at the intervals noted above; however, patients should be carefully monitored and the serum ciprofloxacin concentration should be measured periodically. Peak concentrations (1-2 hours after dosing) should generally range from 2 to 4 mcg/mL.

For patients with changing renal function or for patients with renal impairment and hepatic insufficiency, measurement of serum concentrations of ciprofloxacin will provide additional guidance for adjusting dosage.

HOW SUPPLIED
Cipro® (ciprofloxacin hydrochloride) is available as round, slightly yellowish film-coated tablets containing 250 mg ciprofloxacin. The 250-mg tablet is coded with the word "Miles" on one side and "512" on the reverse side. Cipro® is also available as capsule shaped, slightly yellowish film-coated tablets containing 500 mg or 750 mg ciprofloxacin. The 500-mg tablet is coded with the word "Miles" on one side and "513" on the reverse side; the 750-mg tablet is coded with the word "Miles" on one side and "514" on the reverse side. Available in bottles of 50's, 100's and in Unit Dose packages of 100.

	Strength	NDC Code	Tablet Identification
Bottles of 50:	750 mg	NDC 0026-8514-50	Miles 514
Bottles of 100:	250 mg	NDC 0026-8512-51	Miles 512
	500 mg	NDC 0026-8513-51	Miles 513
Unit Dose Package of 100:	250 mg	NDC 0026-8512-48	Miles 512
	500 mg	NDC 0026-8513-48	Miles 513
	750 mg	NDC 0026-8514-48	Miles 514

Store below 86°F (30°C).

ANIMAL PHARMACOLOGY
Ciprofloxacin and related drugs have been shown to cause arthropathy in immature animals of most species tested (See WARNINGS). Damage of weight bearing joints was observed in juvenile dogs and rats. In young beagles 100 mg/kg ciprofloxacin given daily for 4 weeks, caused degenerative articular changes of the knee joint. At 30 mg/kg the effect on the joint was minimal. In a subsequent study in beagles removal of weight bearing from the joint reduced the lesions but did not totally prevent them.

Crystalluria, sometimes associated with secondary nephropathy, occurs in laboratory animals dosed with ciprofloxacin. This is primarily related to the reduced solubility of ciprofloxacin under alkaline conditions, which predominate in the urine of test animals; in man, crystalluria is rare since human urine is typically acidic. In rhesus monkeys, crystalluria without nephropathy has been noted after single oral doses as low as 5 mg/kg. After 6 months of intravenous dosing at 10 mg/kg/day, no nephropathological changes were noted; however, nephropathy was observed after dosing at 20 mg/kg/day for the same duration.

In dogs, ciprofloxacin at 3 and 10 mg/kg by rapid IV injection (15 sec.) produces pronounced hypotensive effects. These effects are considered to be related to histamine release since they are partially antagonized by pyrilamine, an antihistamine. In rhesus monkeys, rapid IV injection also produces hypotension but the effect in this species is inconsistent and less pronounced.

In mice, concomitant administration of nonsteroidal anti-inflammatory drugs such as fenbufen, phenylbutazone and indomethacin, with quinolones has been reported to enhance the CNS stimulatory effect of quinolones.

Ocular toxicity seen with some related drugs has not been observed in ciprofloxacin-treated animals.

References: 1. Pernet A. Temafloxacin overview. In: *Temafloxacin: A New Standard in Quinolones.* New York, NY: AVMD Group; 1990:1-13. **2.** Phillips I, King A. Comparative activity of the 4-quinolones. *Rev Infect Dis.* 1988;10(suppl 1):S70-S76. **3.** Robbins MJ, Baskerville AJ, Sanghrajka M, et al. Comparative in vitro activity of lomefloxacin, a difluoro-quinolone. *Diagn Microbiol Infect Dis.* 1989;12:65S-76S.

Miles Inc.
Pharmaceutical Division
400 Morgan Lane
West Haven, CT 06516

PZ100735   8/91   Bay o 9867   5202-2-A-U.S.-3   1577
© 1991 Miles Inc.   Printed in USA